YOU CAN'T GIVE VODKA TO A BABY

AND OTHER PARENTING MYTHS

YOU CAN'T GIVE VODKA TO A BABY

AND OTHER PARENTING MYTHS

Dr Oliver Green, B.S.A.

A catalogue record for this book is available from the National Library of New Zealand

ISBN 978-1-927262-26-9

An Upstart Press Book
Published in 2015 by Upstart Press Ltd
B3, 72 Apollo Drive, Rosedale
Auckland, New Zealand
www.upstartpress.co.nz

Reprinted 2015

Printed by Everbest Printing Co. Ltd., China

To my mother and father.
A solid four out of ten.

CONTENTS

WHAT TO EXPECT NOW YOU'RE INFECTED

'Is it always shake a baby or is it never shake a baby?'
'Uh-oh! My baby's a jerk – now what?'

Having questions is a natural part of parenting but finding the right answers without really looking can be difficult. There's a lot of information out there but much of it is conflicting and involves long stints of reading. That's where *You Can't Give Vodka to a Baby* comes in. It is the perfect companion for any new parent, or parents who feel that they have made some horrific mistakes raising previous kids and therefore need a do-over.

Delivered in bite-sized chunks of nutritious information, just like bite-sized chunks of a nutritious Happy Meal, this book will give any parent the advice and confidence to raise their children into adults who *probably* won't end up in jail or on drugs, and to build relationships deeper than any you may have seen on reality TV shows.

I'm Oliver Green BSA and I will share with you my theoretical and untested techniques for dealing with children's manipulative neediness to give a refreshing and often legal take on modern parenting.

BABY WANTED

So you're thinking of having a baby. And why wouldn't you? It's hard to make a real career take off, you're not getting any better looking, your biological clock is chiming louder than Big Ben, and house music and MDMA haven't been good since the nineties. Besides, how hard can it be? Your mother did it, and that was in the days before iPads.

TOP 10 REASONS TO HAVE A BABY

We asked people like you what their reasons for bringing a child into the world were. You'll be touched by what they had to say.

1. I'm bored. *Linda, 32*
2. Our friends are having one so we might as well. *Daisy, 28*
3. Babies are cute to dress up. *Libby, 32*
4. I have the perfect baby name and I want to bagsy it. *Alex, 23*
5. I don't get enough 'likes' on Instagram. *Carol, 33*

6. Reason? Ha! Tequila made that decision for me. *Mary Beth, 37*
7. Beyoncé has one. *Gail, 32*
8. I hate school. *Ellen, 16*
9. I want to eat doughnuts without being judged. *Dorothy, 40*
10. Chicks dig babies, man! *John, 19*

ARE YOU READY TO BE A MOTHER?

Make sure by using this quick questionnaire.

Do you already own enough shoes? **Y/N**
Are your houseplants alive? **Y/N**
Do you know where your house keys are? **Y/N**
Are you wearing underwear? **Y/N**
Do you like saying, 'Don't touch that?' **Y/N**
Do you like wiping things? **Y/N**
Do you wish you could have less sex and laughter in your relationship? **Y/N**
Is spare cash a problem that you'd like to find a remedy for? **Y/N**
Do you like looking at nice clothes but never being able to wear them? **Y/N**
Do you have friends you no longer want to see? **Y/N**

If you answered mostly **YES** to these questions, go, get knocked up and enjoy your new 'life'.

ARE YOU DONE WITH FUN?

You'd better answer this one too.

Do you dance with your hands above your head? **Y/N**
Do you sometimes sleep in your clothes? **Y/N**
Do you know how to do the Macarena? **Y/N**
Do you ever yell, 'This is my jam!'? **Y/N**
Do you know what day it is? **Y/N**
Do you have *both* types of herpes? **Y/N**
Do you have a favourite condom flavour? **Y/N**
Do all your friends have benefits? **Y/N**
Are you hooking-up on Tinder right now? **Y/N**
Is your relationship status, 'It's complicated'? **Y/N**

If you answered mostly **YES** to these questions, you're not done with fun and you're likely to be a mother the courts know about.

WHAT SORT OF BABY WILL YOUR BABY BE?

There are so many different types of baby. Let's discover which type yours will be.

THE 'ACCESSORY' BABY

Put a bow on it. Dress it up. OMG, darling! Get it on Instagram fast. Is it crying? Oh no. It won't stop. 18 years? This isn't cute. Should have got a puppy.

THE 'EVERYONE ELSE IS HAVING ONE' BABY

They're everywhere you look. Everyone's talking about them. You're left out. Nobody wants to play with you. You need a doll too.

THE 'SAVE THE RELATIONSHIP' BABY

Uh-oh! Relationship on the rocks? Try having a baby. Throw a baby onto the inferno that is your relationship and see if it puts out the flames.

THE 'LOST IN LIFE' BABY

Drifting along unsure of what you want in life? Need something to do during the day because you just quit another job? A baby could help.

THE 'I'LL SHOW YOU!' BABY

Dumped by the love of your life? Get pregnant and have some guy's kid. That'll show him! Revenge forever.

YOU WANT A BABY, HUBBY STILL WANTS A LIFE

You're in a committed relationship and you want to have a baby. However, your other half is hesitant. There are a few tried and true ways to get pregnant anyway.

CHEAT

Cheating is the most reliable way of getting pregnant against your partner's wishes. Because you are a woman, you don't even have to try to get sex. Simply go to a place where men are and raise your hand. This will serve as your pick-up line.

LIE

Simply stop taking birth control but — this is the important part — *say* you are still taking them. For example:

Your partner: Are you still taking your contraceptive pills?
You: Yes.

There are many possible variations on this lie. Have fun with it, but remember having minty fresh breath after taking your 'contraceptive pill' is a dead giveaway.

BABY WANTED: ESSENTIAL GEAR LIST

Making a baby requires very little gear. Mostly you just need the gear you were born with to work, which can depend on how much fun you've had and how old your plumbing is.

However, there are a couple of items that can help:

1. Blinkers — put them on now and ignore the dying world that you're bringing a child into.
2. Sperm — you can't make a baby without it, not a human one anyway. If you're lucky, the man you share your life with has some. Supervise him on his laptop while you are trying to conceive. If given the chance, he will waste sperm.
3. Kale — Oh my God, kale! What is kale? I think it's a vegetable but apparently it's AMAAAZING! What the fuck is kale?

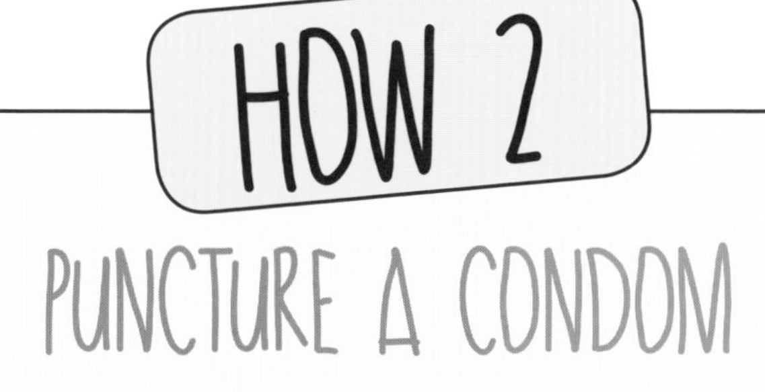

Use a small drill bit. Sperm don't need much room.

4. Antiseptic hand wash — you're going to pee on your hands and fingers more times than you ever thought possible.
5. A sharp knife — to remove your sense of perspective and replace it with a humourless know-it-all version of yourself.

EXERCISE

Those people running or walking very fast down the street aren't trying to escape from the cops. They are 'exercising'. Those people going into large buildings where techno music plays, and a lot of good-looking dudes flail their arms around, saying 'Woo!' aren't drugless raves. They are gyms, and those people are 'exercising'.

YOUR WARRANT OF FIT-LESS

Let's figure out where you stand with this in-no-way-scientific and probably-not-accurate status test.

1. **Can you:**
   Touch your toes? *1 point*
   See your toes? *2 points*
   Feel your toes? *3 points*

2. **Do you lose your breath:**
   Using the stairs? *1 point*
   Using the escalator? *2 points*
   Using the elevator? *3 points*

3. **Do you run:**
   Only when being chased by an animal? *1 point*
   Only when chasing a taxi? *2 points*
   Only when chasing an ice-cream truck? *3 points*

Close to 5 points: You're as ready as you'll ever be.
Close to 10 points: Send out for adoption pamphlets and get some reading done while you convalesce in some sort of clinic.

DIET

Diet is not just a word written on the funny-tasting Coke cans. Nor is it the thing you try to do every year before caving in and buying a bigger bikini. Diet is what you eat and drink, and therefore what your baby eats and drinks. The right diet is crucial for you to be able to photograph food and upload the pictures to social media.

THE UNDERPRIVILEGED TEENAGER'S DIET

Teenagers from underprivileged backgrounds never exercise, they do drugs, smoke and generally treat themselves like skin sacks filled with waste. BUT they do what millions of middle-class women with their yoga pants and quinoa can't do — they get pregnant. Constantly. They have one period — their first — then after that they're basically always pregnant.

Given their prolific breeding ability, the underprivileged teenager's diet plan should be considered for anyone who wants to get pregnant. Let's look at a typical day's diet:

BREAKFAST

1 bong hit
3 cigarettes
1 cup instant coffee with 9 teaspoons of sugar
1 bowl chocolate cereal

LUNCH

1 kg of bite-sized Snickers bars (stolen)
3 painkillers
1 can of silver spray paint (inhaled)
3 litres of fizzy drink
6 fingernails

DINNER

64 sachets of ketchup from an un-named burger chain,
mixed with water to make 'soup'
1 large Hawaiian pizza (taken from delivery guy at knifepoint)
9 bong hits
13 cigarettes
12 cans beer

THE JOYLESS SEX

SEXUAL ADMIN

Sex will become a dull administrative task, like filing or putting the same limp sock into the same drawer over and over and over again. Be prepared to do the often disgusting things men seem to like to keep your guy interested in having sex long after it's become about as much fun as stubbing one's toe . . . on a vagina.

THE HORROR OF SOBER SEX

For many of us sex is something that happens with copious amounts of alcohol. In fact, the word COPULATE comes from the word COPIOUS as in 'Before we copulate I would like to drink copious amounts of alcohol . . .'

Quite rightly as it's fraught with embarrassing noises and silly faces. But baby-making sex is a sober affair that requires darkness and background noise. Music works but the women I interviewed reported that Ryan Gosling movies had a better effect.

☆TOP TIPS☆

BABY CUSTOMISATION

You customise your sofa, your running shoes and even your car. Why not customise your baby? Studies show Asian babies with French accents are the cutest of all babies and the good news is your baby could be that cute.

There are literally billions of Asian people (you might be one) and all you have to do to have an Asian baby is have sex with an Asian man. Studies show you might not even feel it. Make your baby tall, short, athletic, bookish — it all depends on who the customisation male is.

HOW DOES IT WORK?

Tall man = Tall baby
Strong man = Strong baby
Ugly man = Baby with a good sense of humour
Immaculate man who likes to talk = Gay baby
Rich man = Nanny's baby

DEALING WITH THE PENIS WHILE SOBER

The penis is a ridiculous and ugly-looking thing. Mine either looks like a bald one-eyed weightlifter, or a shrivelled elephant's trunk left to dry up on the sands of a vast pubic-haired desert. The best way to deal with a penis when sober is to squint when looking at it — in that way it can look like a chicken leg or a puppy's squeaky toy. Also try lying on your arm for 20 minutes — this should numb your hand totally making touching the ridiculous thing possible.

TEN POSITIONS THAT GUARANTEE MALE ORGASM

For years some questioned the existence of the elusive male orgasm. However, science has revealed that the male orgasm does exist, and there are a few sure-fire sexual positions that will guarantee that it occurs during lovemaking.

1. The three-car pile-up
2. The escaped tuna sinks a kayak
3. The steeple builder's concern
4. The curious worm
5. The burning village waits for snow
6. The pork puzzle
7. The chain gang escapes
8. The angry snake ruins a picnic
9. The chimp with a handgun
10. The last cookie gets crumbled

HANGOVERS

NATURE'S PREGNANCY TESTS

Pregnancy tests are expensive, and there's a good chance you may pee on your own fingers, which is beyond revolting. A fun way of discovering whether you are pregnant is with wine. Drinking heavily is not only a great way to get pregnant, it's also nature's pregnancy test.

Use the following handy chart to see if you're with child, and what potential damage may have been done to your foetus.

Congrats. You're having a mentally challenged baby.

0–3 UNITS CONSUMED

Hangover is like your brain has been Rodney Kinged by racist police = **PREGNANT**

3–6 UNITS CONSUMED

Hangover is screaming at you like a house fire at an orphanage = **PREGNANT**

6–9 UNITS CONSUMED

Hangover is like a beaker of acid spilled into a barrel of rattle snakes and cats = **PREGNANT**

9–12 UNITS CONSUMED

Hangover is like a falling out of the fun-tree and hitting your face on every thorn-covered branch on the way to the rocky ground = **PREGNANT**

12–30 UNITS CONSUMED

Have you ever seen a pickle jar with only one pickle floating in it? That's your baby now. **SEEK MEDICAL ATTENTION**

THE MIRACLE OF WHAT'S NOT HAPPENING INSIDE YOU

So you're still not pregnant. Time to hit the internet and start looking for unproven, sometimes Mexican, fertility treatments. Crystals? Sure. Lizard blood? Why not? How about something crazy like fostering a kid over the age of three?

TIME TO FACE THE FUN INFERTILITY FACTS

Here are some facts about TTC (trying to conceive), which is AUPA (another unnecessary pregnancy acronym).

1. Infertility is defined as the inability to conceive after 12 months of unprotected sex. Or, for married couples, six intercourse sessions, whichever comes first.
2. As you get older, conception becomes more difficult. This is because fewer men want to have sex with you.
3. Sperm can survive in the body for six days by engaging in cannibalism and gladiatorial practices. Sperm fight and eat each other until there is only one giant sperm left standing on the carcasses of millions of dead sperm . . . but by then that sperm is often too big to move so it dies of obesity-related disease. **Fact.**
4. Stress, poor diet, alcohol abuse, being overweight, being underweight, too much exercise, or not enough exercise all cause infertility. It seems likely that the only people that can have babies are other babies.

HOW 2

MAKE DOLLS HOUSE OUT OF NEGATIVE PREGNANCY TESTS

Look! A dolls house. Haunted with the sadness of infertility.

GAME ON

THE INFERTILITY BLAME GAME

During the infertility journey, the time will come when it's necessary to dish out blame. When that happens it's important to know the rules of 'The Infertility Blame Game. A game for two players.'

SET-UP

1. Both players exhaust all options trying to get pregnant for months.
2. Chew through savings and, if possible, go into debt going through multiple rounds of IVF.
3. Stop talking to each other entirely for 3–7 days.
4. Choose a nice restaurant to have some 'time together that isn't about babies'.
5. Drink at least one bottle of wine.

ROUND 1: At the restaurant

PLAYER 1 — begin by questioning whether ***PLAYER 2*** should be drinking.
5 points

PLAYER 2 — start yelling, 'You think it's my fault, don't you?'
10 points

PLAYER 1 — responds by yelling, 'How could you say that? I've done nothing but be supportive!'
5 points

PLAYER 2 — initiates actual blame. 'Maybe if you hadn't smoked pot right through your twenties you wouldn't have such lethargic sperm!'
10 points

PLAYER 1 — comes back strong. 'Maybe if you weren't such a dried-up bitch your womb wouldn't be a desert.'
10 points

Players now score 5 points per introduction of the following terms: *wizened, mama's boy, husk, tiny penis, deep regret, divorce, secretary, loser, frigid, weak genes.*

YOU'RE DOING IT WRONG

Another possibility for not being able to conceive is that you may be doing the whole thing wrong.

ON YOU NOT IN YOU

Sperm will not reach your egg if they start their journey on your stomach.

Check: Can you see the semen after ejaculation?
If yes: You're doing it wrong.

SWALLOWING

Sperm will not reach the egg by swimming down your oesophagus. It will meet a fiery death in your stomach acid.

Check: Can you taste the semen after ejaculation?
If yes: You're doing it wrong.

INTO A TEST TUBE

Simply getting someone to ejaculate into a test tube will not get you a test-tube baby. If your partner is attempting to ejaculate into a test tube, this is reason enough to never have children with him.

Check: Are you having sex in a lab?
If yes: You're doing it wrong.

TIME TO GIVE UP

One or both of you has a sour, broken, deficient body that won't make life. Rather than take that as nature telling you that you are deficient in some way, you should continue on your manic quest to own a human being.

TICK-TOCK, TIME TO ADOPT, CHIMES THE BROKEN, OLD BIOLOGICAL CLOCK

Adopting a child is a great way to both get the baby you've been obsessing about and to help a drug-addled, wayward young mother get back onto the streets as quickly as possible.

Even though you have a mortgage and a three-year-old Audi, adopting a newborn baby is surprisingly difficult, whereas adopting an older child is easy. Newborn babies are more likely to become little clones of you, whereas older children are the sum parts of all the terrible human beings they have encountered on their hellish slide through life thus far.

Believe it or not there's a waiting list for healthy not very crack-addicted babies and this list is difficult to get on and unless you live somewhere bribe-y like Russia, or are part of a homosexual power couple, it's going to be hard to get a baby. Here are some other ways to get yourself a human life:

BABY FACTORY WANTED — THE SURROGATE MOTHER MACHINE

Surrogacy is when you pay a woman to carry your baby for you and then wrench it out of her arms in the delivery room, then give her a couple of grand and a restraining order.

BECOME THE CRAZY AUNT

You can't have kids but your sister or brother can. Sure you're bitter. Sure you're angry. But don't give in to those feelings — instead be bat-shit crazy.

Day trips without permission: Pick the little ones up during school for a fun trip 'just driving and crying' with their aunt.

Totally inappropriate gifts: Boys like guns, right? Girls like horses, right?

Breastfeeding: Just because the toddler isn't yours doesn't mean you can't breastfeed it. Not legally anyway.

Renaming the child: The child is named Elizabeth but that doesn't suit her. She should have been named Violet. Just call the child Violet. Violet likes you more than her silly old parents anyway.

THE SWINGS AND ROUNDABOUTS OF ADOPTING AN OLDER CHILD

Oh shit! You are desperate. Adopting an older child means that you have tried everything else and that you are probably allergic to cats. There's nothing like hearing your child's first words even if they're, 'Shut up, you're not my real mother!'

KIDLESS COUPLES: CAN YOUR MARRIAGE SURVIVE 'NO KIDS'?

You can always tell the middle-aged people with no kids – they're the ones on the train quietly brainstorming topics of conversation for the coming evening and carefully pacing out the episodes of box-sets so that 'the silence' doesn't edge into the room and reveal the fact that from here on in it's just book clubs, travelling in matching tracksuits, and dying in front of each other for entertainment.

Here are some things childless couples like you have done to keep things spicy:

AFFAIRS

A sure way to keep a childless marriage interesting is to have an affair. Men look no further than a work colleague. Women try the husband of a good friend. Both of these options are tried and tested and will give you something to talk about in the coming days.

DIVORCE

Dividing up matrimonial property is always a fun thing for childless couples to do especially with the help of expensive lawyers.

YOU ARE A SEX WORKER

A man and a woman have approximately 10,000 sexual encounters together before the whole thing just gets old and dies. Making a baby burns through your allotted fun 'weekend sex' encounters and races you towards the 'Wednesday sex' that should be waiting for you in your middle age.

The longer it takes to conceive the less fun sex becomes. Eventually you will see yourself as a sex worker, and sex will be like going to a job at a vagina every day. Sex becomes a chore. Something to get through rather than enjoy. So to make sure you get the job done as quickly as possible: it doesn't have to be fancy, it just has to be quick.

LET'S GET WEIRD

One great thing about finally being the one who is pestered for sex is that you have a little more sway in the bedroom. Your wife is more likely to entertain any weird sexual quirks you have if it means sex to completion is forthcoming twice a day. If you like weird shit, now's the time to ask for it. Want your butthole tickled with a feather? Ask. Want her to hiss like a snake? She'll probably do it.

ARE YOUR SWIMMERS ONLY GOING TO QUALIFY FOR THE SPECIAL OLYMPICS?

It's not just women that need to prepare their bodies for conception. Men need to do their part too. Luckily your contribution begins and ends with ejaculation. To make sure you are providing a healthy set of swimmers, here are some top tips:

1. **Keep testicles cool** — While at your desk at work or while sitting at a restaurant simply remove your testicles from boxers or briefs and let them be at room temperature.
2. **Avoid testicle trauma** — Does this need to be spelled out? You should be avoiding testicle trauma, regardless of whether you're trying to get someone pregnant. Why aren't you avoiding testicle trauma? Avoid the shit out of it. It's traumatic.

TOP TIPS: HOW NOT TO MASTURBATE WHEN TRYING TO CONCEIVE

Not masturbating is a must when trying to conceive. You can't waste sperm in tissues, socks or pot plants. You might be throwing away a future professional athlete and your pension.

1. Don't be left home alone for more than nine minutes.
2. Don't be bored for more than three minutes.
3. Don't shower unsupervised and even then don't wash your genitals.
4. Don't look at a friend's wife's beach holiday photos.
5. Only go on the internet at crowded cafés.

YOU'RE PREGNANT

Maybe you've planned it like a modern couple, maybe it was an accident 1970s style, or maybe you were just trying on a swimsuit in a secondhand store — the truth is it doesn't matter how you fell pregnant, all that matters is that the life you used to know is over and your new life is about to begin. Because there'll be a lot of vomit, tears, some blood, and a thing called the mucus plug, but it'll all be worth it once you have a whole other person that you OWN.

WOBBLES AND WORRIES

Will I be a good mother? Will I remember to feed the baby? What if I lose the baby in a nightclub? All natural concerns with simple answers. We all have some concerns — don't worry you are NOT alone. All women have these feelings. Here are a few wobbles with some calming answers.

WILL I HAVE TO WEAR UGLY JEANS FOR NINE MONTHS?

Yes. Good jeans for pregnant women have still not been invented. It's no exaggeration to say that your next nine months will be crimes against denim. Teams of denim researchers have worked tirelessly to make you look like a Russian shotputter in her father's dungarees.

WILL I HAVE A GINGER CHILD?

Just over 0.5 per cent of children are born ginger, but this no longer has to mean a life of hardship. Many ginger children grow up to lead normal lives and find outlets for their freakish strength, small tail-like appendages, and ability to speak to otters.

WILL MY HUSBAND STAY THE SAME WEIGHT?

Yes. But your weight will increase dramatically. This is because you are doing all the work and he is doing nothing. The only thing you can do is keep putting beer in the refrigerator. Nothing kills a six-pack like a six-pack.

WILL I BE A GOOD MOTHER?

Most definitely – sometimes. The best your child can hope for is a childhood slightly better than your childhood. If you were locked in a cupboard for being disobedient, you should aim to lock your kids in a walk-in wardrobe.

TREND ALERT

BABY NAMES THAT MAKE YOU SOUND FAMOUS

Celebs and famous people aren't naming their children Tom or Charles or Tabitha any more. They are being 'creative' by giving their children the names of places, fruit, towns of conception, and sometimes whole sentences. To keep up, you need to think more like you're naming a restaurant, a boat or a racehorse. Let your imagination soar.

BOYS

- Liquorice
- Winter Wind
- Bollard
- Sofa by the Window
- Captain Mordor
- Special FX
- The Child formerly known as Keith
- Haircut
- Tiny Bits

GIRLS

- Pepper Mill
- Summer Breeze
- The letter Q
- Nice Scarf
- Bellini
- Hooker with a Heart
- Anyone's Guess
- Compost
- The same as Gwyneth's

BUY THE SEX OF BABY YOU WANT

The best way to influence the sex of the baby is to spend money on it. Simply go and drop thousands on a pink nursery, pink crib, pink diamond tiara and you'll have a boy. Then raise your boy as a girl and create yourself an interesting minority that will keep you entertained into your retirement and might get you invited to a dinner party or an art gallery opening.

HOW NOT TO START A BABY BLOG

Not starting a baby blog is easy. There are many blogging platforms on the web that are perfect to not use to not start your baby blog. No one wants to hear about any renovations you might be doing to your baby's room or see photos of any cute booties or hats so don't include them when you're not updating your baby blog. Also you'll be eating healthy now so make sure you're not sharing pointless pictures of kale and quinoa.

Not starting a baby blog is a great way of not constantly talking about your pregnancy. There are so many fun things you can avoid putting on the blog you are not starting.

NO fun belly selfies.
NO fun thoughts on baby names.
NO fun quotes for other mothers.
NO recipes for yummy healthy snacks.

The main thing to remember is not starting a baby blog should be enjoyable for you as well as a relief for your friends and family. Happy not blogging!

FIRST TRIMESTER (WEEKS 1–12)

THE TERRIBLE TRIMESTER

The first trimester is totally pointless and annoying. You are as sick as a junkie and look like an alcoholic, but can't enjoy any drugs or booze. Plus you can't tell anyone you're pregnant so no one is going to call you 'AAAAMMAAAAAAZZZING!' and give any more of a toss about you than they already don't.

Stabby Feelings: You'll feel like taking a knife and making holes in people. A good remedy for this is to wear mittens and only carry a foldout pocketknife.

Craving Listerine: You'll start craving and eating weird things, which will be reflected in your disgusting breath. Pickle juice on ice-cream smells like yesterday's feet.

Throw up a lot AND gain weight: It's called morning sickness because it's always morning somewhere. You'll throw up a lot but, unlike your favourite actress, you won't get 'bikini summer body' skinny. You'll get 'harpoon her and drag her onboard' fat.

UNDERSTANDING THE SIZE OF YOUR BABY

Let's put it in terms you'll understand by comparing them to things in your life.

1–3 weeks: the size of a cigarette butt
3–6 weeks: the size of a shot glass
6–9 weeks: the size of a $20 tinny of weed
9–12 weeks: the size of a minibar bottle of booze

THROWING PEOPLE OFF THE SCENT

Your friends will all be trying to guess whether you're pregnant. As soon as you aren't drinking wine out of a chipped tea-cup at 2 am in some random kitchen, they'll guess you're with child. You will be asked many questions, but here are some sure-fire ways to throw them off course.

Q. Why have you been seeing a doctor?
A. I'm dying.

Q. Why aren't you drinking?
A. Alcoholism. This morning I woke up with a tramp pissing into my shoes.

Q. Why are you throwing up all the time?
A. West African burrowing worm. It jumps.

Q. Why have you got pregnancy tests?
A. Kleptomania. This isn't my purse.

TWELVE WEEKS

IT'S FINALLY ABOUT YOU!

Twelve weeks is the most special time in a woman's life . . . because you get to tell everyone and it really becomes all about you.

STATUS UPDATE

Your status update is too long. The maximum status length is 420 characters, but it is 2300 characters long.

OKAY

GIVING BIRTH TO YOUR 'UNIQUE' AND 'SPECIAL' NEWS

Here comes a special, unique announcement that only 125 billion women have made over the history of humanity. You've done something so unique and special that it only happens once every minute, on the minute, every day of the year, forever.

MILK FIVE DAYS OF STATUS UPDATES OUT

Day 1 — The quizzical status that forces friends to ask for more information. Example: Who says good things can't come out of a bottle of $8 wine?

Day 2 — Pile on the mystique, but give them a little hint. Example: I'm going to miss putting soft cheese on oysters.

Day 3 — More hinting. More mystique. Something classy. Example: My gynaecologist has the coldest wristwatch.

Day 4 — Post the scan shot. This is the Hiroshima moment. BOOM. No need to say anything.

Day 5 — The encore. Keep the conversation going. Example: Does he look cute enough to keep? Not sure. #adoption

GETTING YOUR PREGNANCY INTO ANY AND EVERY CONVERSATION

As a newly pregnant mother you need to learn how to make any conversation about your pregnancy. Here are a couple of examples of how to get it done in two simple steps.

Conversation starter: Did you hear about that mine collapse in Peru that trapped 200 miners?
Your response: Oh that's terrible . . . I have a minor inside me.

Conversation starter: I just got fired.
Your response: Look on the bright side. I'm pregnant.

Conversation starter: My aunt just died of cancer.
Your response: BABY!!! INSIDE!!! ME!!!!

NUTRITION

EATING, DRINKING AND SMOKING FOR TWO

Your baby eats what you eat. In fact it eats you. Like a tiny cannibal. I don't know the science exactly, but there's a tube connected to the baby that all the chewed-up food goes through, or something. Your job is to throw things into your mouth for the tube to deliver. Weird things. Lots of things. But always two of everything.

CRAVINGS: BABY MIND CONTROL?

I have heard tales of women eating coal, pinecones and even eggs benedict without hollandaise sauce. The horror. Science hasn't found the cause of cravings, so I'm filling in the blanks here. Cravings are your baby being an asshole.

Your baby thinks of something foul — like wool and camembert — and then using baby-mind-magic makes you want to eat that. It's all for the baby's amusement but might also be used as punishment for minor infractions like moving during the night and having organs.

BABY LITE: SMOKING DURING PREGNANCY

Smoking during pregnancy can cause babies to be premature and underweight. But look on the bright side, a pack a day will help keep the weight off, and ensure a birth you probably won't even notice long before you're bored with being pregnant. You get a baby that's hand-held, purse-sized and easy to handle, as soon as the tubes come out and it can breathe on its own.

Quit quitting: If you're trying to quit smoking, give up. It's harder than quitting heroin. If you do heroin, the good news is that it's easier to quit than cigarettes.

How to start smoking.

1. Find a brand of cigarettes you like the look of — if you're still throwing up a lot try menthol to cover your dead man's breath.
2. Do a budget and see what vitamins you don't need — smoking isn't cheap.
3. Start puffing. It will make you sick at first but stick with it. Start smoking as soon as you wake up and then every hour after that.
4. When you feel like you need a cigarette you're done. Welcome to addiction.

Congratulations! You'll be meeting that tiny, tiny, tiny baby much sooner than you thought.

CAFFEINE

Caffeine is a stimulant, which gives you the gift of more hours in the day by causing insomnia. Coffee is liquid procrastination and then it's liquid panic. It's why you have 10 Word documents and 32 webpages open, and you have six to-do lists that all start with . . . WRITE TO-DO LIST.

Caffeine makes babies dance: Coffee is like giving your baby a little workout inside you. A couple of espressos and your little one can really stretch its cashew-nut-sized legs and zumba the shit out of your bladder and liver. Remember, an active baby is a baby born with toned arms and six-pack — who wouldn't want that?

ALCOHOL

Alcohol relaxes babies and makes them more fun to be around. It's a great way for a baby to lose its inhibitions. All the great parenting stories start with, 'After the third shot of tequila . . .' None of them start with, 'Then we switched off the DVD and went to bed.'

FOOD

THE COMFORT FOOD PYRAMID

The Comfort Food Pyramid is a pyramid comprised of the foods that work like an anti-anxiety medication. The following is a breakdown of the groups that make up the Comfort Food Pyramid:

The pastry group
The chocolate-covered group
The deep-fried family
The mystery meats

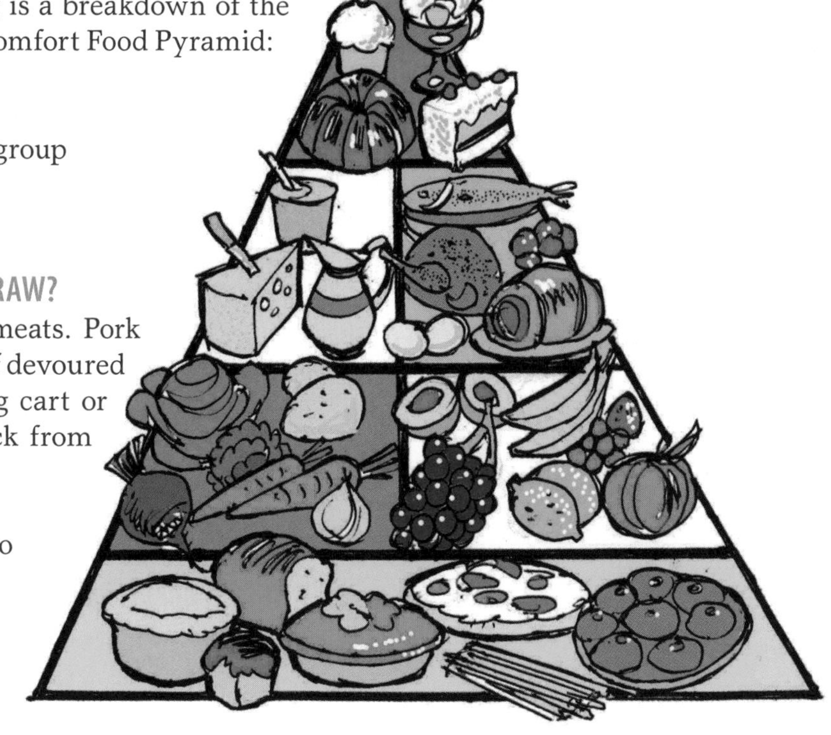

WHAT MEAT CAN BE EATEN RAW?

It's advisable to cook all meats. Pork and chicken may kill you if devoured straight from the shopping cart or in the car on the way back from the supermarket.

NB: Human meat falls into the pork family. Although delicious, human being needs to be cooked and the meat hidden.

VITAMINS

Vitamin C, D, B2 or, as I call them, 'the generic vitamins' are okay for normal people but as a pregnant woman you need a little extra. The following are lesser-known but equally important vitamins.

VITAMIN TV

Everyone knows that the sun provides us with vitamin D, but few people know that reality TV gives pregnant women much-needed vitamin TV. Not to be consumed on an empty stomach.

VITAMIN O

Vitamin O comes specifically from food stolen from other people's plates. Best found in restaurant situations.

VITAMIN J

Vitamin J is found in the jam filling in doughnuts and cookies. Good for staining clothing and making fingers sticky.

VITAMIN S

Vitamin S comes from secret food that you have hidden away from judging eyes. Possible hiding places include your tumble dryer, garden shed or body cavities. To extract the full benefit of vitamin S, the food is best consumed whilst crying.

HOW 2

DEAL WITH DUMB PEOPLE WHO WON'T JUST SHUT THE HELL UP

STEP 1
Embrace the dark hatred inside your soul

STEP 2
Make the world a better place.

MOOD

It's your motherfucking hormones! They're running around your brain looting and stealing. You have no hope of controlling them so don't even bother trying.

RECOGNISING THE TRIGGERS

Knowing what will set your mood from stun to kill is important unless you want to raise your child alone after everyone you know and love has drawn a line through your name on their Christmas card list, or they are languishing dead at the bottom of a pit covered in lime . . . where you threw them. Look for the following common triggers:

Days ending in the letter Y
People's faces being all facey

COMMUNICATION

Letting people know how you feel with your words is key to finding a way through your 'heightened' moods. Experts call this communication. The problem with communication is that it is often not very hurtful and it seldom punishes the person you are communicating with.

Sometimes actually talking to people runs the risk of them talking back, which could cause you to scratch their eyes out. That's where writing messages on the mirror comes into its own. Wake up early and let everyone know what's in store for the day.

Keep them short: DON'T TALK TO ME

Or longer: TALK TO ME AND I WILL CUT YOUR FAT FACE OFF YOUR SKULL

They can be for work: WHOEVER KEEPS USING THE MICROWAVE AND LETTING IT BEEEEEEP IS DYING TODAY

They can be for those you love: KEEP SNORING AND I'M TAKING A FINGER WITH A STEAK KNIFE

SECOND TRIMESTER (WEEKS 13–28)

THE 'BYE-BYE BODY' TRIMESTER

Parasites often make the host organism sick before killing it. The infestation starts slowly but eventually the parasite starts to take over the host, leeching the nutrients from their food, the energy from their muscles, and the light from their eyes. Babies are like that. The second trimester is the one where your body goes from 'You want to make a baby all up in me don't you?' to 'Put down the harpoon – I'M A HUMAN WOMAN!'

STRETCH MARKS

Imagine you are a birthday balloon. Now imagine you are a birthday balloon under the couch. Now imagine you are the birthday balloon under the couch a week later, deflated and sagging.

PATCHES OF DARK SKIN ON THE FACE

This is sometimes called the pregnancy mask. Be careful when you enter banks as you may be pre-emptively shot or tackled by security guards.

ITCHY PALMS OR SOLES OF FEET

Itchy feet are likely to drive you insane. One method for dealing with this constant itching is to wrap a cricket stump in barbed wire. This makes an excellent foot scratcher that can be kept in your car, next to your sofa, or on a handy rope around your neck.

YOU HAVE FAT ANKLES — YOU HAVE FANKLES

Wear high heels and your feet will look like sausages. Take your rings off now or lose them in the folds of newly swollen phalanges. Get ready for some sticky questions at passport control when you go on holiday because you look like a fat version of you that ate the skinny version of you. And that holiday, make it a skiing holiday. A bikini would make you look like a roast chicken.

NINE WAYS TO WEAR SWEATPANTS

Sweatpants are a pregnant woman's best friend. You'll live in them. The savvy preggy fashionista knows how to get the most out of them. Here are some top looks to S T R E T C H your sweats further.

1. Cut your sweats off at the knees for the summer months.
2. Drop stew on your sweatpants for a one-off-customised look.
3. Pair your sweatpants with a nice blouse for Skype calls with friends.
4. Cover your sweats in glitter glue for an evening-wear look.
5. Try to force some cowboy boots onto your swollen feet for something more 'fashion forward'.
6. Put other sweatpants over the top of your sweatpants to save washing.
7. Stitch denim pieces onto your sweatpants for the most comfortable 'jeans' in the world.
8. Hack your sweatpants into a skirt for a formal occasion.
9. Put your sweatpants in the blender for a few seconds and create that 'fish net' look for a night out.

BOOBS

If there's one thing good about being pregnant it's two things. Your boobs are your best asset and need to be displayed prominently if you have any chance of distracting people from your puffy, rash-infested pregnancy 'glow'.

Enjoy your boobs before you have an infant swinging on them like an orang-utan on a tyre, turning them into alsatian's ears.

THE BOOB WINDOW

There's a window where you have boobs but no bump. If you come from a background of having tits like a nine-year-old boy this will be an amazing time. You will finally understand the pathetic nature of men, and you will be able to walk around all day with a cornflake stuck to your chin without anyone noticing.

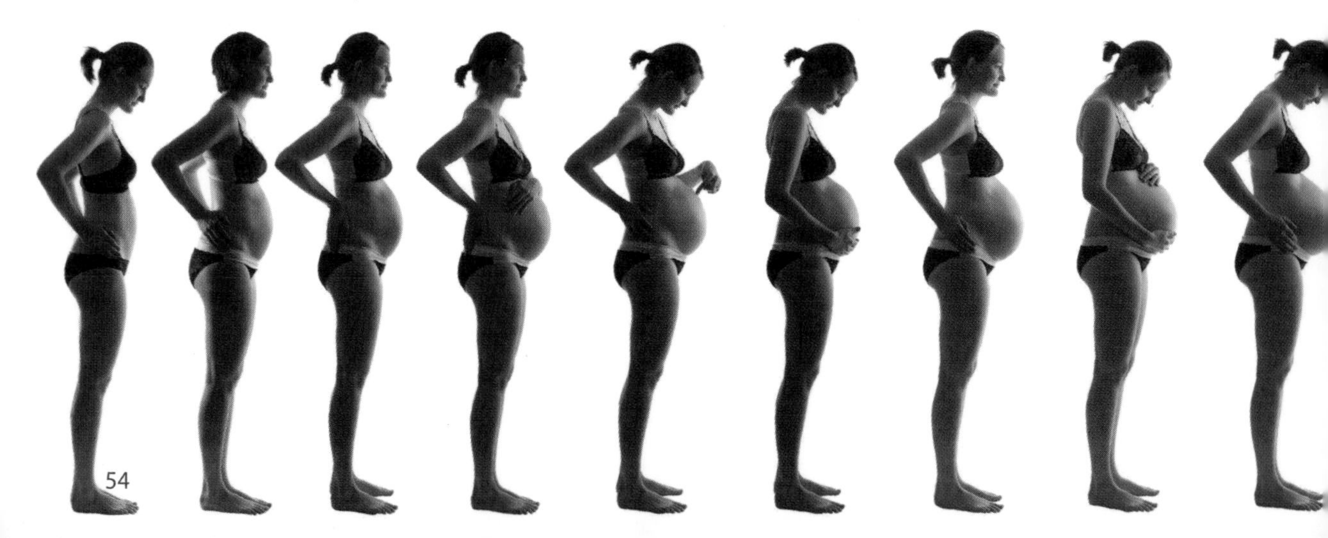

SIZE OF BOOBS AS RELATED TO WHAT YOU CAN GET AWAY WITH

Because the world is still basically run by men who like guns, the police force is 99 per cent male. This means your new boobs are the ticket to a crime spree. It also means you'll be able to engage in the social no-no's that would have normally seen scorn heaped upon you. Here's what you can expect to get away with:

B cup — Littering, singing on public transport while wearing headphones.
C–D cup — Jay walking, back-to-back chick flicks.
D–DD cup — Speeding, calling a policeman a nincompoop.
E–EE cup — Grievous bodily harm, remote-control dominance.
F–G cup — Genocide, double-denim.

SEX DURING PREGNANCY

Some women get as horny as a Wimbledon ball boy working a Williams sisters match, while other women get as hornless as the last hunted unicorn. Whatever you are currently feeling, remember there are two people in your relationship so you'll have to deal with it/him somehow.

BEST POSITIONS FOR NOT HAVING SEX

Not having sex while pregnant can be a rewarding and beautiful experience for both of you. There are so many rewarding positions for not having sex to keep you both unsatisfied during the loooooong nine months it takes to grow a baby that, once born, will also stop you having sex.

The car lock: She locks herself in the car. He stands outside pleading.

The 1000-piece puzzle: She does a complex jigsaw puzzle. He tries to guess what it is.

The infomercial watcher: She stays up until 2 am watching TV saying, 'I just wanna see the end of this.' He goes to bed alone.

The mother's staying: She invites her mother to stay. He sulks a bit and does the washing up a lot.

BEST POSITIONS THAT WON'T CRUSH YOUR HUSBAND

At the other end of the spectrum, you're a raging animal filled with hormones – unfortunately the animal is a baby hippopotamus. Crushing and killing your husband is a very real possibility. Here are some positions that will keep hubby safe and you satisfied.

The email: She sends him a provocative shot. He takes his tablet to the toilet for some 'me time'.

The reversing truck: She reverses slowly into position.
He nervously shouts directions.

The jab and move: She acts like George Foreman. He acts like Mohammed Ali in his prime.

THIRD TRIMESTER (WEEKS 29-40)

THE 'GET IT OUT OF ME' TRIMESTER

MASSIVENESS

You are huge. That pregnancy glow is now a skin-melting inferno. People feel sorry for you. People fetch you the 'sturdy' chair. Your biggest fear is falling over, not because you'll damage the baby, but because you'll never be able to get up again.

HAEMORRHOIDS

You are so big you are starting to turn inside out! Your insides are starting to reveal themselves in a burning, itchy fashion. These are called 'maternity luggage' and you'll carry them wherever you go, probably forever.

LEAKING BREASTS

Your giant swollen boobs feel like they are going to burst. However, they will not burst as nature has a way of relieving pressure — constantly dribbling like an insane man on Thorazine eating pudding.

EXTREME PAIN

Pain will visit you like it has never visited before. Searing hot pain. Dull thudding pain. Tearing shooting pain. All the pain. They say by focusing on your happy place you can divert your mind from the pain. This is bullshit. The only way this works is if your happy place has a giant needle filled with anaesthetic being pushed into your spine.

BABY COMING OUT OF YOUR VAGINA

This is a defining feature of the third trimester. Near the end of your nine months a live person will come out of your vagina and into the world. At that point you will no longer be pregnant, you will be a parent.

ARE YOU COMPLAINING ENOUGH?

As a pregnant woman you should be getting at least three uninterrupted hours of complaining done per day. Spreading the three hours out over the course of the day is the surest way to let those around you know that you are doing this alone and they are a bunch of dead weights dragging you down.

MAKING THE MOST OF YOUR HIGH-PITCHED VOICE

In addition to the wonders of swelling and your face changing, pregnant women's voices are known to rise a whole octave. This is to amplify your complaining and constant weird demands. The high-pitched nature of your new voice will cut through any background peace and quiet and make sure you are the centre of attention as soon as your mouth is empty enough to whine.

INCREASING THE VOLUME OF YOUR SIGHS

Sighing is a great way to let the people round you know that you are dissatisfied. Room temperature, the wrong room? Water too wet? By sighing you can wake sleeping husbands and alert uncaring friends on cellphone calls that you need . . . something.

YOU CAN BE A TOTAL BITCH NOW

Being heavily pregnant allows you many privileges including being a total bitch. Now is the time to tell everyone exactly what you think of them. Don't pull punches.

New mother, Jennifer, 28, tells us about being honest with people. 'It was great. I just told them all what I thought of them, then sent texts later saying that I was pregnant and hormonal.

'It was great fun. Really great stress relief. Even now I've had the baby I sometimes stuff a pillow up my jumper, drive around and just yell at people out of my car.'

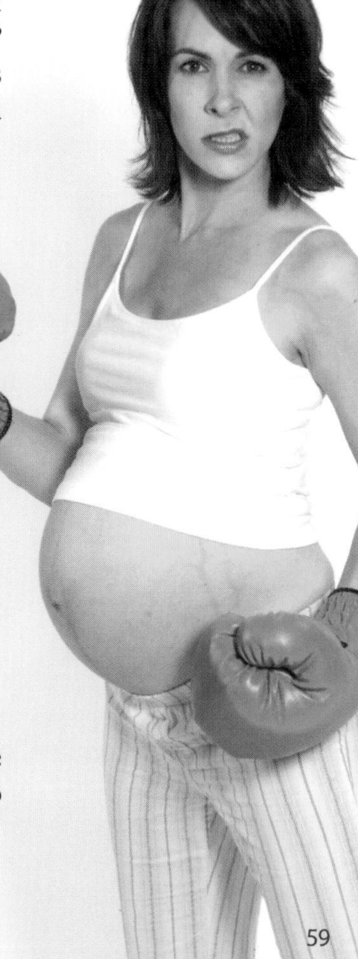

THE WORLD IS YOUR TOILET

When nature calls, it doesn't leave a message. Can you see the toilet from where you are? Then move. You will need to go to the toilet all the time.

IN THE WOMB

Right now in your womb your baby is plotting its release. The havoc it will cause and the misery it will unleash on you depends on the information you let slip while it gains strength and waits for the right time to burst out of you and take your world hostage.

IN UTERO GENE TESTING

Testing for defects in the womb is possible and encouraged. Discovering that your child could grow up to be a jerk as an adult and preparing for that eventuality is the least you can do — for the rest of us.

Goth gene: The goth gene can now be detected but not eliminated. This at least leaves you with options for raising your goth. There have been some incredible advances in halting gothness using therapy and balloon animals. Whatever you do, don't despair — it will only encourage the darkness in your goth child.

Country music gene: Loving country music is a disease that, if caught early enough, can be stopped in its tracks. Therapy includes playing rap music to your unborn foetus and banning ill-fitting denim from the house after birth.

Caucasian with dreadlocks gene: This serious defect affects a small number of Caucasian people. It's never okay for a white person to have dreadlocks. Knowing that dreadlocks could be coming lets you prepare for disowning your child in later life or shaving the child's head while it sleeps. Remember, every time a white person grows dreads a real Rasta dies.

PREPARING FOR THE BIG MOMENT

It's time. The moment you've been dreading for months . . . or weeks if you are one of those people who don't know they're pregnant until their waters break that we see on the news sometimes and think, 'What the actual fuck?!' It's time to unplug the mucus plug. It's go time, people!

LOOK EVERYONE! IT'S YOUR VAGINA!

Unless you're Australian, you're probably not used to a whole lot of people seeing your vagina. Well, that needs to change. A great way to get used to a room full of people looking at your vagina is to show people your vagina. By showing your vagina to as many people as possible you'll be ready when the big day comes.

Take a photo of your vagina.

Add it to an email and press 'reply all' on as many emails as possible.

Wait for the reaction. This will start the process of readying yourself for the big show.

OVERDUE BABY

They say it's better to have an overdue baby than a premature baby, which is true unless you're the one waiting for the thing to come out.

WHY IS YOUR BABY REFUSING TO COME OUT?

There are many reasons your baby isn't coming out. Here are the most common ones:

It's realised it's all downhill from here.
It's lost in your massive womb.
It's not finished demolishing you from the inside.
It's got everything just how it likes it.
You're not pregnant after all — it's just gas.
The kid hates surprise parties.
It looks like shit and knows there'll be cameras.
Fashion dictates lateness.
The father has been singing to it with an acoustic guitar.
It's heard your Australian accent.

MAKE A BIRTH PLAN

HOME BIRTHS AND BIRTHS THAT AREN'T REALLY GROSS

Giving birth is a completely natural process that is really, really disgusting. Most people who give birth end up covered in blood, faeces and sweat. Here are some ways to make birth less horrific than gutting a live deer.

Airbnb.com: Holiday home rental websites are a great way to have a home birth without making your own home into a hall of horrors.

Hugh Hefner's spa pool: A birthing pool is a lot like a party at the Playboy mansion. You splash around a bit and after a while a wrinkly wet thing comes to the surface of the pool.

The Hollywood: This could be your last chance to be really high for a long time so take the Lindsay Lohan approach and come to a couple of days later with a baby, a hangover, zero chance of a movie career and the knowledge that a bunch of people you kind of know have seen your butthole.

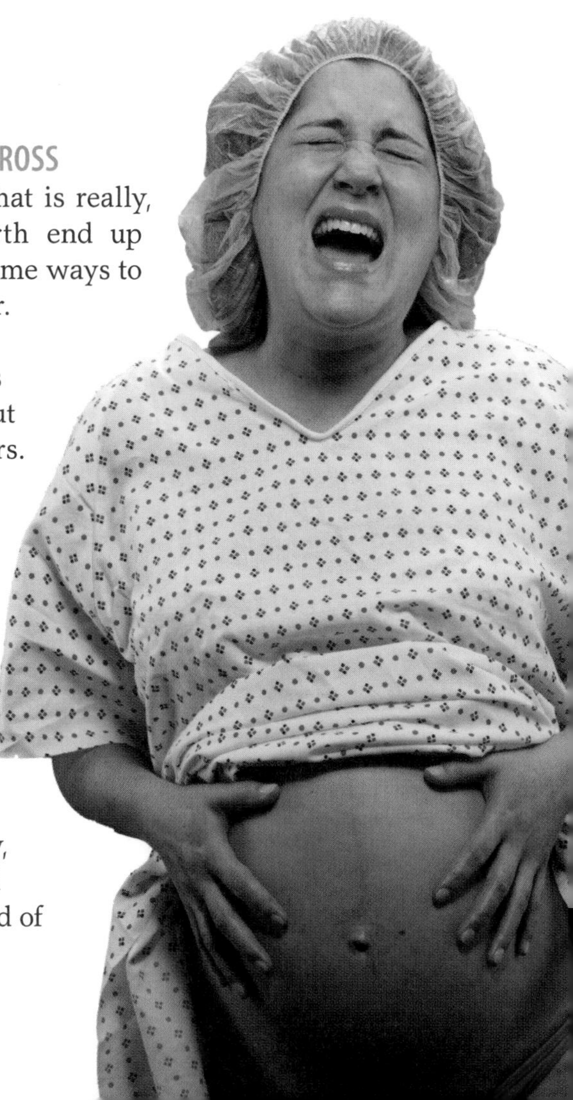

REAL-LIFE STORY

MY HUSBAND DIED DURING CHILDBIRTH

During the birth of our twins, my husband tragically got his stupid head caved in with a bat. He was saying stupid things like, 'We're doing great!' We? WE? And there he was standing next to me wearing crocs! WE were having a home birth and WE kept a baseball bat by the bed so I reached out, grabbed it and accidentally stoved his head in with it.

Linda, 34, London

GO TIME!

Mike Tyson once said, 'Everyone has a strategy until I punch them in the face.' This is never truer than when you are giving birth. So plan all you want. Tell everyone what you're going to do and how you'll do it . . . and then when it starts call Mike Tyson and beg him to come and punch you in the face.

ALTERNATIVE PAIN CONTROL (ALTERNATIVE TO THE ONES THAT WORK)

Aromatherapy: Basic rule: if it comes in a needle, it works. If it comes with a wick, it's horseshit.

Acupuncture: The needle part is right but apart from that, it's wrong. Look around you. Do you really need another useless prick in your life?

Massage: Unless you're massaging the plunger of a hypodermic syringe, don't bother.

Meditation: 'Oh look a baby just came out of me and I didn't notice because I was meditating,' said no one ever.

Breathing: Inhale peace . . . Exhale a torrent of threats.

When it's go time, it's time to go. Nothing in the world is going to stop that little thing from bursting out of you. Here's what to expect:

FIRST STAGE

Contractions start. Or 'a shortening of the uterine muscles starts.' This feels bad, but save the hysterics. You'll need them later. This is where your birth plan starts flipping you the bird. Early contractions are just a little tickle of the log-splitting pain that's hurtling down the pipe at you.

Early on, your cervix is dilating. It's getting out of the way because a bowling ball is about to come down the bendy straw. At this point you'll get a thick, stringy, blood-tinged discharge called the bloody show. As in 'For fuck's sake, start the bloody show!' Here are some things people will tell you to do:

Take a shower or bath
Listen to relaxing music
Have a gentle massage
Try slow, deep breathing
Drink water, juice or other clear liquids
Eat light, healthy snacks
Apply ice packs or heat to your lower back

None of that shit helps. At all.

SECOND STAGE

Here it comes. There's nothing you can do about it now. Lean into it, but remember to yell, 'No photos of my butthole!' At this point, if you have your birthing plan written down on paper, tearing that useless document into shreds may help deal with your anger.

Swearing relief: Swearing is the one thing that can really help. Truly effective swearing requires stringing as many expletives together as possible. It also helps if you direct the swearing at someone. This also gives your husband a reason for being there, apart from the 10 hours of vending machine raiding that he's been doing up to this point. Some effective examples of swearing:

1. Fuck as every word in the sentence: 'F***ing f*** you f***ity f***ing f***errrrrrrrr!'
2. Your husband is a *&@@#: 'You did this you prick-smoking mama's boy shit-sucking f***tarrrrrdddddddd!'
3. God is a $$%&*: 'Bastard, f*** God? Why you shit-licking, dress-wearing cloud Nancy. Butt-sniffing, omnipotent f*** snake. Why this way? Why not eggggggggggsssss?!'

THE FIRST HOUR

In the 1950s everything was better. Baby was born, was removed from mothers and taken to a debriefing room where it was deloused, perfumed, squashed into a decent shape and brought back to the mother ready to be looked at through a window. Clean. Easy. Civilised. But now the whole thing has gone touchy-feely interactive and the baby is handed straight to the mother still covered in the gunk that kept it alive. It truly is a backward step towards the cave days. What's the point of having $500,000 worth of equipment surrounding you and then being handed a slippery little gunk puddle with eyes and grasping little fingers?

SKIN ON SKIN TIME OR 'GET ME THAT' TIME

Skin on skin is important for the development of your baby. Bonding. Love. Closeness blah blah. Sure. But it's more important for you. It's when you realise that your baby lying on top of you means that you can't get the things you want and need and will never have to go through the almost peasant-like hassle of getting them yourself. The first hour of your baby's life will herald a new stage in your life known as the GET ME THAT stage. It's when the world comes to you like you're magic. Put a sleeping baby on your lap and you're like Harry Potter.

OH, THAT'S WHAT BOOBS ARE ACTUALLY FOR

Immediately your baby will start eating you through your breasts. This will give you an aha moment when you realise that your boobs are actually for feeding a tiny human not for jamming into bikini tops, holding up strapless dresses or for your husband to do that weird thing with his tongue he thinks you think feels good – but doesn't.

LET'S LOOK AT YOUR NEWBORN

No baby is born perfect. At least – no baby of yours. You'll be handed your newborn and you'll start to see the flaws almost immediately. Here are some common problems and some simple solutions.

BABY LOOKS LIKE AN ANGRY, WRINKLED SCROTUM

Your baby won't always look like a scrotum — it will start to look like a bizarre mix of you and your husband. But, while it does look like a scrotum, try to love it anyway as research shows that babies who are not loved end up as serial killers and politicians.

BABY IS BORN DIFFERENT ETHNICTY

Having a baby that comes out a different race to you or your husband can **be awkward. If baby does come out an ethnicity your husband was not expecting try focusing on the positives. 'You've always wanted a boy.' Or 'At least it's not retarded.'**

BABY LOOKS LIKE TINY APE

Babies are born with a covering of hair all over their bodies called a 'lanugo' which is something I didn't make up. It's real. It's either because we are descended from apes or if you are Christian you just gave birth to an actual ape. Deal with it.

BABY HAS GIGANTIC TESTICLES

Baby boys are born with gigantic balls. These will shrink to normal size but while they are big don't forget to take photos of them. Great for first meetings with first girlfriends.

BABY LOOKS LIKE IT HAS NO FACE JUST A LONG VERTICAL SLIT FOR A MOUTH AND LEGS COMING OUT OF ITS HEAD

Your baby is upside down. Hand it back to the nurse and ask for adoption papers.

SAVE YOURSELF — DESTROY THE EVIDENCE

If you're one of those couples who takes photos of everything that happens in your crappy lives and, while you were pushing a human out, your husband was snapping away mumbling about the aperture and trying to capture some 'essence' — then now is the time to do the edit. Make your first words 'Honey, give me the fucking camera!' Do it now. Do it for the rest of us.

Before Shots: This is the least problematic time. Especially if you keep the photos to nine months before . . . if you insist — keep these shoulders and above and in between contractions.

During Shots: These are the shots nobody wants to see. Nobody. They are crime scene shots. Horror movie photos.

After Shots: Acceptable but only after the baby has been 1950-ised. Cleaned, powdered and perfumed.

PLACENTA DELIVERY

The final stage of the delivery is the placenta slithering out of you. If you have a dream catcher above your bed, and you're about to name your child after an animal, this is a meaningful stage for you, your husband and wolf. For everyone else it's just more birthing grossness.

PLACENTA RECIPES

You just gave birth and boy are you hungry! Like all mammals your baby was also a delivery person bringing you a meal — the placenta. Placenta eating is gaining popularity especially amongst loopy white people who have too much money, time on their hands and need to have something to one-up other crazy white people with at dinner parties. Here are some quick and easy recipe ideas:

Placenta stew — Great for a winter evening. Why not invite someone who can read auras so you can share your placenta with them for karma's sake. Add red wine and sweet potato for a rustic twist.

Placenta frites — A French classic. Fry the placenta, add salt and pepper, and serve with thin fries.

Placenta Bolognese — Your husband knows how to make a Bolognese right? It's the one dish he can cook. Add onions, tomatoes and a pinch of 'holy shit we are eating a part of me'.

WHAT WILL YOU PASS ON TO YOUR CHILD?

You cannonballed into the gene pool with all your clothes on. What do you expect? You're going to make a splash. Look at yourself. You are like the rest of us. Average. This means that your baby has already got its inheritance.

Baldness: 45 per cent likelihood
Alcoholism: 33 per cent likelihood
Laziness: 56 per cent likelihood
Inability to dance: 43 per cent likelihood
Love of action movies: 53 per cent likelihood

SOME TOPICS YOU'LL PROBABLY NEVER GET TO DISCUSS AGAIN

If you like talking about anything other than babies, get it all in now. Consider recording these final conversations so you can replay them later:

Favourite sandwich fillings
The weather
The dog you once loved
Your hopes and dreams
Adults you know that don't have babies

NO. 1 DAD MUG: AN INDUSTRY BASED ON FEAR

'Big Mug' is engaged in a conspiracy aimed at fathers just like you — their aim is to coerce men into a behaviour that the Mama Mafia deems as 'good'. Your reward for this behaviour? A mug. You tell me — who's the mug? Don't fall for this scam. The No. 1 Dad mug should be shunned as a badge of shame.

YOUR NEWBORN

It may take time to get used to the fact that newborns are very self-absorbed. They're just all 'me, me, me'. Luckily, you have one thing in common – all either of you really care about is food and sleep. Use this as an opportunity to ignore everything else in the world and bond with your mini-you. Just don't forget to set your DVR because you'll have the baby for a very long time but this season of *My Kitchen Rules* will only last for a few weeks.

THE BASICS

Who's got time to read a whole five pages on newborns? Not you, clearly. So here's all you need to know about raising a newborn in two minutes. Tear the next page out and stick it on the door of your refrigerator.

Feed — Your newborn will be hungry a lot but can't eat 'people food' just yet. That stuff leaking out of your new giant boobs is what it eats. Let it latch on like a leech and it will be happy.

Sleep — Newborns sleep a lot except when you want to sleep. They wait until you are asleep before they wake up.

Me me me — Newborns are hugely self-centred. They only want to do what they want to do. This makes them hard to like. If you find yourself not liking your newborn, put sunglasses on it and draw a moustache or beard on it.

Advice — Ignoring advice is a skill every new mother needs to have. You'll find advice coming at you from everywhere. Most of it encourages risk-averse and coddling behaviour. A brilliant way to ignore advice is to shut all doors, and switch off phones and laptops. If you find that you are still getting advice from actual faces, just remember the key phrase, **'Shut up, you nasty old woman.'**

Dull — All babies are dull. They are terrible conversationalists with conservative worldviews and zero interest in doing much. Instead of making your baby more interesting, nature has a way of dumbing you down to stop you from leaving your baby for a dog to raise.

If it ain't pooing, eating or crying, call the nurse - This is the golden rule if keeping your newborn alive is something you definitely want to do. If it's not doing something annoying, call a nurse.

TAKING BABY HOME

A SPECIAL TIME (TO FREAK OUT)

This is it. Your baby is yours. As you wave goodbye to the safety of the hospital and its drug-resistant strains of disease, you'll realise that it's time to actually raise the child. This is when you should start to really freak out. In addition to worrying aimlessly, here are some things to really shit yourself about.

ARE YOU WORRYING ENOUGH? ARE YOU? ARE YOU? JESUS! ARE YOU?

All new parents worry. But worrying affects mothers more than fathers because, studies show, mothers love their children up to 30 per cent more than fathers do. Let's be frank, at first fathers are just like, 'Fake it 'til you make it.' Some of your concerns are silly (but not many — so be concerned) and should be ignored but others are very, very real and should be worried about intensely.

TAKING THE WORRY OUT OF WORRYING

Lots of new parents worry that other people might be worrying more than them, or that maybe they aren't worrying effectively enough. A great way to make sure you are worrying enough and at the right intensity is to set aside 45 minutes at the beginning of every hour for a good fret. Ask yourself — Are you on the verge of tears? Can you feel your heartbeat? Is there sweat pooling in the palms of your hands? Are your teeth grinding? If you answer No to these questions, you might not be parenting.

NEWBORN ON A BUDGET

Children are expensive. Apparently it will cost you $500,000 by the time your child leaves home . . . or $100 if you decide to dump the baby in a supermarket fruit and vege section early — less if you take a bus there and back. Here are some ideas to help you save money with your newborn:

CONVERTING A CAT BED INTO A COT

It wasn't long ago that your pets were alive but, now that your cat is a taxidermied doorstop, its bed can be vacuumed and used as a cot for your new baby.

CONVERTING A GYM BAG INTO A CARRY COT

You won't need that gym bag with the sturdy handles any more. Simply use your expensive gym clothes to line the inside of the gym bag and you've made a practical carry cot for your new little excuse not to get fit.

DON'T BOTHER BUYING A CAR SEAT

Just take the empty bladders from wine casks, inflate them and tape them to the baby's limbs and precious skull. Any car accident will see the baby bounce around rather than being crushed.

SOCKS AS CLOTHES

Baby clothes are expensive and babies grow out of them fast. Save money with your newborn by using a series of socks instead of clothes. By stuffing your little one into a sock and then putting a second sock on their head you'll save hundreds.

MEH, IT'S PROBABLY NORMAL

Seriously. Who knows what's normal? None of the experts have a clue and everyone with a baby is constantly lying about the experience. Here are some out-and-out guesses about what is 'normal'.

MISPLACING THE BABY — NORMAL

Can't find your baby? Don't worry, it happens all the time and often won't result in criminal proceedings if you find the baby as quickly as possible.

MOST COURTS WANT TO KNOW THAT YOU MADE AN EFFORT TO LOOK IN THE FOLLOWING PLACES:

1. In the trunk of your car
2. In the refrigerator
3. Being sniffed by some dogs somewhere
4. In the dog's bed (also check you aren't breastfeeding the dog)
5. Down the back of the couch
6. Still at the hospital
7. At a grandparent's house
8. Under the table at a café
9. With adoptive parents
10. At lost and found in the mall

STALKING YOUR NEWBORN — NORMAL

Many new mothers are just creepy and a little bit stalkery. They won't stop talking about their baby and tend to stare at it a little too long. It's creepy. Take this quick questionnaire to discover if you are stalking your newborn:

Are you watching your baby sleep? **Y/N**
Are you smelling your baby right now? **Y/N**
Are you saying things like 'I love you', even though you have just met? **Y/N**
Are you telling the baby how to dress or actually dressing it? **Y/N**
Do you insist on knowing the whereabouts of the baby the whole time? **Y/N**

If you answered mostly Yes to these questions you may be stalking your baby. It might be time to let up on the reins and give the kid some space.

HIDING YOUR REAL FEELINGS

Many people will ask you how you are feeling. They don't want to know. They are just being polite. Just hand them your baby and smile. There's a good chance that everyone in your house is going through hell – you, your baby and what's-his-name.

It's natural to feel a little down after the birth of your baby, because you just punted your whole life away. Suffering in silence is a sure way not to spread the depression to other people. Hiding symptoms can be as simple as lying, cutting yourself off from friends, or simply staying in a dark room. Don't let your depression bum others out. *Crush that feeling into a pain diamond.*

YOU FEEL LIKE THE WORST MOTHER EVER

This is a natural feeling and it doesn't mean that you are the worst mother ever. You might just be a shitty one. Don't worry too much. The baby won't remember much until they're about three so unless you scar the thing, you'll be fine.

YOU FEEL LIKE YOU'RE OVER IT ALREADY

It's been three days and you're already looking for a nanny to take the worm thing off your hands. How well do you really know the child? Now would be a good time to make the break, if you're going to make it.

CRYING ALL THE TIME: YOU AND YOUR BABY HAVE SOMETHING IN COMMON

Crying is one of the only things that your newborn can do with any real proficiency. Rather than learn a new skill like fetching the remote or just shutting up for 10 minutes, your newborn will tend to do what it's good at. Wailing.

Seriously, what the fuck is colic? If your baby is suffering from colic, you'll soon realise that scientists are idiots and they should all be piled high on a fire. No one knows what colic is, only that it was sent from God to punish mothers and make their lives hell. Colic, or chronic crying, has no cure.

WHAT DO THE CRIES MEAN?

Newborns are attention seekers, yes, but it also turns out they are also judgmental and harshly critical. No one knows for sure what a baby's cry means, but here are some semi-educated hunches:

Long drawn-out screams with slight upward inflection: Disappointed with its surroundings – specifically interior design choices. May hate 'bunny wabbits'.

Short stabbing outbursts of fury: Fearful for its future and your ability to provide a balanced and worldly viewpoint.

Huge inhalation of breath followed by high-pitched siren sound: Anger at being forced to wear hand-me-down baby grows.

SOME THINGS TO TRY WITH A CRYING NEWBORN

Parenting a newborn has less to do with knowledge and love, and more to do with knowing a few simple tricks. Here are some mostly legal tricks for dealing with the unceasing cries of your newborn:

Singing: You have to sing really loud though. Babies' cries are shrill and you need volume to drown them out.

White noise: Try playing white noise through headphones. This should drown the sound of anything out.

Fireworks: If not used carefully fireworks can permanently damage hearing. Be sure to read the instructions and then do the opposite.

Happy place: Learn to disassociate from your surroundings. Tortured POWs in World War II talked of being able to remove their minds from their bodies and thereby endure terrible trauma by going to a 'happy place'.

Busy: A busy newborn is a happy newborn. Keep your baby busy with small but rewarding tasks – gutting a fish, sorting screws, gardening.

Going for a long drive: This works every time unless you bring the baby with you, in which case it's about 50/50.

Drinking: If drinking can help you get through meetings and other people's weddings, it can help you with your baby's crying too. Try to stay conscious however, in case of a house fire.

Auto tune: It works for pop stars with zero talent and a voice like a stepped-on puppy. Try running your baby's cries through an auto tuner and give it that metallic robot sound that made will.i.am the annoying megastar he is today.

SWADDLING STOPS CRYING

Swaddling is a great way to comfort yourself and stop your baby crying. To be clear — your baby will remain crying but you won't be able to hear it because of the swaddling.

1. Choose a thick piece of cloth or blanket.
2. Wrap it around your whole head layering it on the ears.
3. Leave breathing holes and a hole for the mouth.
4. Nap.

HOSPITAL RETURNS

Although your newborn seems defective and may be outright broken, it isn't. It's just doing what babies do: very little — and what little it does is annoying. The hospital isn't like a shopping mall — they won't let you bring the baby back. However, that doesn't mean you can't try. I have developed a return system I call the 'Five D's'.

Disguise: This is important as there are cameras everywhere. Don't be too flamboyant. Try painter's overalls and a dust mask — hospitals are always being patched up.

Daytime: The best time to return the baby is during visiting hours. The hospital is busy at this point and they probably won't notice one more person carrying a package.

Delivery: Head straight to the delivery room area of the hospital. This is where your baby looks the most normal.

Dump: Remove the baby from the tool bag or other smuggling device and dump it in the nursery where the other babies are.

Dupe: You're not a monster. You want your baby to be raised well, so look for a nice family and simply switch the nametags on the cots. This way your baby will be taken home from the hospital and probably not returned.

BREASTFEEDING

Breastfeeding is nature's way of making people around you uncomfortable while saving you money on baby food. It's also a brilliant way of meeting perverts and teenaged boys. But mostly it's a good way to watch a lot of TV.

BREASTFEEDING PROBLEMS

Breastfeeding isn't always easy. You have boobs. The baby has a mouth. You are the food. The baby is hungry. You'd think nothing could stop the little bald vampire from eating you, like a pissed-up rugby team in a curry house. Sometimes there are problems attaching or not attaching as the case may be.

Baby makes creepy eye contact: Babies make suspect eye contact when breastfeeding. Try and ignore the baby, but if it keeps staring employ sunglasses on either you or baby. NB: Babies in sunglasses are hilarious.

Baby makes sucking noises that drown out my 'stories': The only thing for it is to turn up the volume on the TV. Missing crucial moments in your 'stories' is a sure route to postpartum depression.

Baby thinks my milk is gross: If your baby throws up after feeding, it could be because your milk tastes gross. You never knew you had a flavour but you do and evidently you taste TERRIBLE. Time to start thinking of yourself as a mamaccino and add some flavour by snorting a line of cinnamon.

MIDDLE EASTERN BREASTFEEDING TENT

If you want to hide your breasts from bus passengers or some guy who takes the table next to you at the café as soon as your boob comes out, the Middle Eastern Breastfeeding Tent could be right for you.

THE BREASTFEEDING POSITIONS

Finding the right position for you and your baby can be done by trial and error. Sometimes your ungrateful newborn won't latch on and you might have to switch it up to keep it exciting.

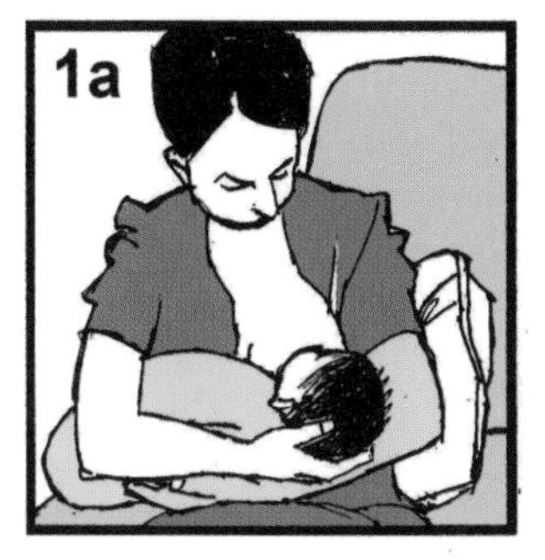

POSTION 1a
The 'Vice Lord Wants What The Vice Lord Wants'

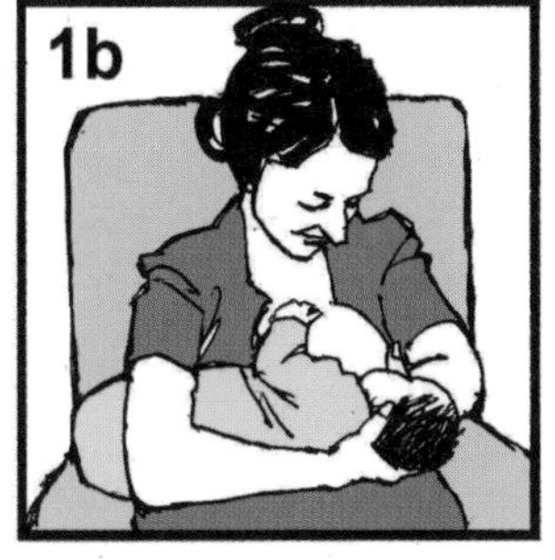

POSTION 1b
The 'Leech with opposable thumbs'

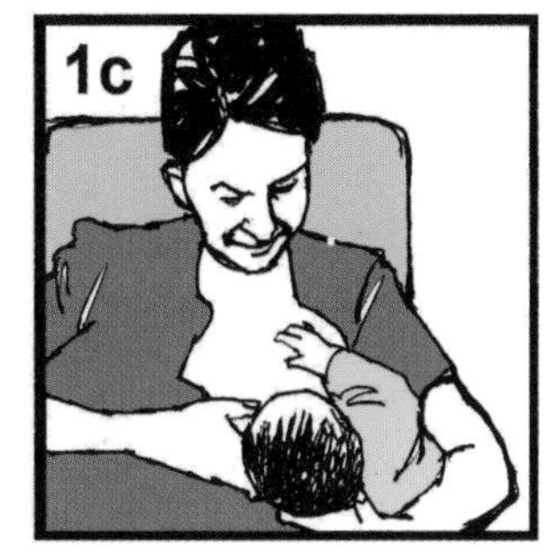

POSTION 1c
The 'Politician Outstays his Welcome'

BOTTLE FEEDING

The main benefit of bottle feeding is that someone who isn't you can do it. This means you can go and do whatever you want, whenever you want. There are some downsides to bottle feeding around nutrition, disease, bonding and actually seeing your baby grow. But then again . . . movies and popcorn. Know what I'm saying?

SLEEP

Remember when not sleeping was caused by being out having fun? Now it's always because you are a 24-hour milkmart. Sleep now seems like a dream, which is a cruel, cruel irony. Unfortunately, sleep is linked to 'not being crazy' so you need to have some sleep or you can expect to 'start being crazy'.

BEDTIME ROUTINE

Teaching baby a good bedtime routine is vital. This can go wrong if parents rush through the steps in an attempt to get their baby to sleep as quickly as possible. However, there are some simple DOs and DON'Ts:

DO put baby to bed at the same time every day. Most parents opt for half past can't-take-any-more-of-this.
DON'T go to bed before your baby does.

DO tire your little one out first. Dancing around the room or horsey riding or abandoning baby to her bouncer while you go and let your 'grape juice' breathe.
DON'T try to use the Spock pinch from *Star Trek*.

DO remove any bruise-covering make-up you might have put on the baby over the course of the day.
DON'T lick the child clean like a mother lion.

DO discuss the events of the day. Maybe you saw a doggie, which was huge news. This may need to be discussed further.
DON'T just laugh maniacally while you shake your head and pound your fists on the table.

DO get any grievances with baby's attitude or behaviour off your chest — it's never good to go to sleep on an argument. An open and honest discussion with your little one works wonders.
DON'T be bullied into holding your tongue. Take a rattle and call it the 'rattle of truth'. Whoever holds the rattle has the floor and should not be interrupted.

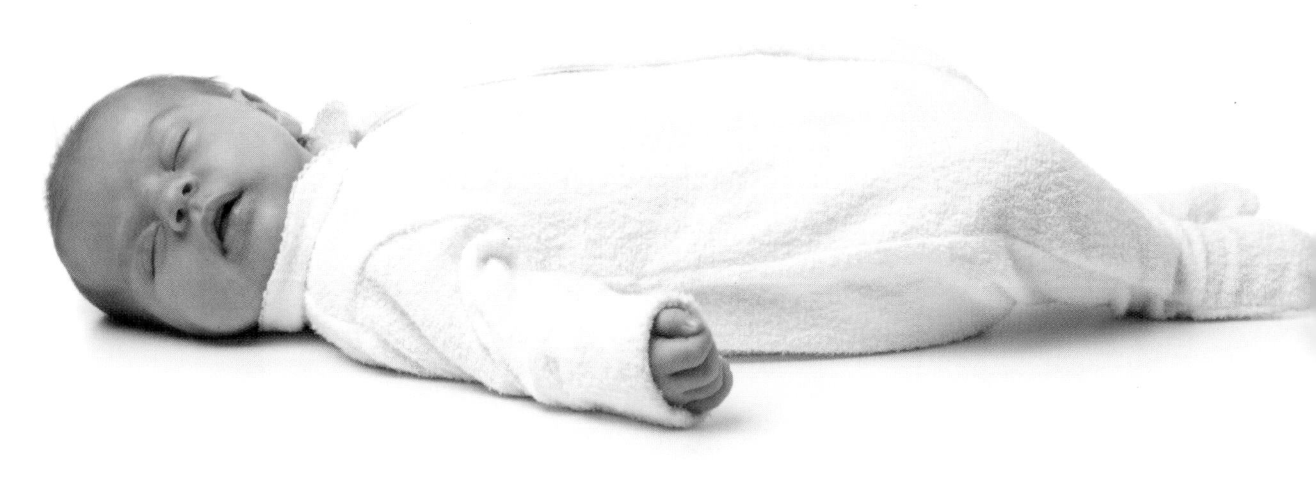

DO play some gentle music. If baby wakes up, you are less likely to hear it cry. Metallica is good.
DON'T wake baby up with your crying. Keep the music at a volume that will drown your cries out too.

SURE-FIRE WAYS TO GET YOUR BABY TO WAKE UP

Waking a baby is easy when you know how. It doesn't take much effort at all. In fact, the smallest infraction will do it.

Sighing: Tough day? Big sigh . . . Great. Now your day's not over.

Breathing quietly in the next room: Breathing quietly is like a jackhammer to a baby. Congrats more baby time.

Resting your head on a pillow: Looks like you're lying down. If you want to sleep, then your baby will be wide awake.

THE GENEVA CONVENTION AS IT RELATES TO YOUR NEWBORN

Your newborn could be behaving like a war criminal. The Geneva Convention clearly states no 'cruel and unusual punishment'. Meaning no torture. Sleep is vital to your sanity and well-being. Sleep deprivation is a common torture tool that will eventually break anyone, no matter how tough they are and how well they are trained. It's used by ruthless regimes and by newborn babies who have only one goal — forcing a Stockholm syndrome situation where you are brainwashed into loving the infant.

FIVE WAYS TO STAY AWAKE DURING THE DAY

Staying awake is crucial for doing things like driving a car or operating an oven. Here are some sure-fire ways to stay awake:

Hot coffee: dripping into your crotch.

Exercise: like running away.

Driving: the risk of death should keep you alert.

Flailing around on the floor.

Crime: become a victim of mugging. Fighting for your life will stop the snoozy feeling.

FIVE WAYS TO ENJOY THE HIGH OF SLEEP DEPRIVATION

You're never going to sleep again, so you might as well try to find the bright side of sleep deprivation. Here are a few great ideas for entertaining yourself when it gets so bad you feel like you're on fun drugs:

1. Scribble on your feet and genitals with a pen.
2. Listen to some techno music and flick the lights off and on.
3. Try to follow a Spanish-language soap opera.
4. Call sport talkback radio and do an impression of your baby crying.
5. Test-drive a motorcycle.

OH SHIT – IT'S POO

The first poo after the baby is born will be a mess. It will get in places you never thought possible, and it will look like nothing you've ever seen. You'll need a lot of wipes and a strong stomach. Remember it's natural and it won't ever be that terrible again. And the baby's first poo might be bad too.

BABY'S POO

The first poo your baby does is a great moment that you will want to commemorate. It will be all too soon before your baby grows up, turns five and is sent away to boarding school. With that in mind, here are some great ways to keep that first poo forever.

Poo painting: Why not use the poo to paint a picture of the poo?

Bronzed poo: Collect the poo in a Tupperware container and send it off for bronzing.

Freezer poo: Keeping the poo in the freezer is a simple way of being able to relive the poo whenever you're feeling nostalgic. Let the poo melt a little and the smell should take you back to those magical first days.

Poo tattoo: Nothing says 'I love you' like a tattoo of your baby's first poo. Most tattoo artists are fine working with a photograph. Just make sure you see some of their other work before you commit. You don't want it to look like shit.

DIAPERS

CLOTH OR DISPOSABLE?

You may have to wear diapers for the first couple of months until your undercarriage is rebuilt. This will stop unnecessary leakage and what doctors don't call 'snail trail', but if they did it would be apt. Here are the pros and cons of cloth diapers versus disposable diapers.

CLOTH DIAPERS

Pros: Can choose denim or another cloth that matches your blouse.
Cons: Will have to wash own faeces out of diaper.

DISPOSABLE DIAPERS

Pros: No washing. Easy to change. Little bunnies and teddies on the packaging are quite cute.
Cons: Will have to buy them at the supermarket with a straight face.

IT JUST LIES THERE AND SLEEPS: DEALING WITH THE DOUCHE THAT GOT YOU PREGNANT

Your partner got you into this mess, and now it's time for him to help with the mess. He'll be tired and want to sleep, eat and whinge. This is a no-no. Motivating your DH (Darling Husband — another UPA) is not an easy feat. The usual threat of leaving him doesn't work in these situations, because that's probably what he wants. Instead, try these simple threats:

USE GOOGLE SEARCHES AS A VEILED THREAT

Go to the family computer and use Google to let him know how you feel. If he's like most men, the only clean thing in his life will be the search history on his laptop. Next time he finishes 'working' in the home office, he'll see your little . . . note — the following search strings.

POISON > TASTELESS > UNTRACEBALE
CLEANING A CHAINSAW
VAN RENTAL
MAP OF WOODLAND
TICKETS TO ARGENTINA

CIRCUMCISE YOUR SON AS A VEILED THREAT

If you decide to circumcise your baby boy, use this as an opportunity to strike fear in the heart of your husband. This fear should bring him into line.

Make sure you maintain eye contact with your husband throughout the entire procedure. Smile.

Ask the doctor where he got his surgical gear, then 'Will a kitchen knife work just as well?' Produce kitchen knife from pocket.

Ask the doctor if there are some YouTube videos you can watch. Watch videos on laptop in bed later.

Nine months ago you had an orgasm that you can't remember and went 50/50 on a baby. Now it's time to 'be a father' and usher your newborn into babyhood, toddlerdom, childhood, adolescence and adulthood — without adding another jerk to the jerk pile. Fatherhood is like the pair of XXL sweat-pants you'll soon buy — something you grow into. Unlike your amazing partner it's not something instinctive, so for the first weeks your goal should be 'don't kill it'.

SHE'S JUST NOT THAT INTO YOU

Your baby won't know you even exist for months. You don't actually matter yet. If this were a football match, you'd be bringing the oranges at half-time. If it was *Star Wars*, you would be an Ewok. If it was a wrestling match, you wouldn't have a fancy name. You'd be Barry and on the receiving end of a dropkick. Your baby will always bond with its mother first. Studies show that you should be bringing something — why aren't you bringing something? That's all you're good for.

ABB — ALWAYS BE BRINGING

Like your dad and his dad before him, you are now part of a proud tradition of fetching things. Fetching is what dads like you are good for. Fetch a bottle. Fetch a blanket. Fetch some soup. Although these might seem like easy tasks, you will get them wrong because you are not psychic and also because you are a stupid jerk. The key to fetching well is that you should never bring just one thing. Instead you should always fetch multiple things. If you are sent for a blanket, bring a blanket and a cup of tea. If fetching a pillow also bring a box-set.

NEWBORN BABY DRINKING GAME

Being so unimportant in the early stages of your child's life leaves you some time for secret drinking. The following are the rules for the Newborn Baby Secret Drinking Game.

1. Every time your wife says, 'Hold her head', you do a secret shot.
2. Every time your wife says, 'I'll do it', you skull a beer.
3. If asked if you're drunk and you don't reply, 'Yeah, I'm drunk. Like I'd be drunk with our new baby . . .' you do a penalty shot with beer chaser.
4. If you drop the baby, skull a beer then leave home.

YOUR BABY

Your baby is not a newborn any more. Your baby will finally be cute, which may help you not want to stuff it back where it came from. Your relationship will be entering a nice numb zombie trance-like stage, which will stop the need for talking or any physical contact.

Even though your baby is growing it's still pretty much useless. Let's look at your baby and try to find something it can actually do apart from looking like a tiny conservative.

ONE MONTH

At four weeks, babies can mimic your face. If you have a 'bitchy resting face' this is a trait that can be passed on to your child. You may start to recognise your own looks in your baby. Especially:

1. Pained
2. Overwhelmed
3. Distraught
4. Desperate
5. Lonely

TWO MONTHS

Baby can grip things that are handed to it, making it a useful cigarette holder. Baby can also smirk at you while you change its poo-filled diapers.

THREE MONTHS

Baby can be placed on its stomach and will lift its head. Useless really. Maybe paint it black with boot polish and make it do a seal impersonation for the internet.

FOUR MONTHS

Baby can recognise your face but will still prefer to look at your boobs. 'Hello. My face is up here!'

FIVE MONTHS

Baby can hold its own head up without flopping all over the place. So you'd better call the mayor and tell him to dust off the parade floats. Baby can also amuse himself by playing with his hands and feet, making him a lot like someone on mushrooms.

SIX MONTHS

Baby starts cutting teeth. Time to think about weaning or melting wax onto your nipples.

SEVEN MONTHS

Baby says first words – probably 'Mama' because Dada is not really pulling his weight. Also because you keep saying, 'Say Mama. Go on. Say Mama. Ma . . . Ma!'

EIGHT MONTHS

Baby can wave goodbye, making divorce that much tougher on one of you. Baby can point at the thing or person it wants. Again, divorce will be hell for one of you.

NINE MONTHS

Baby is crawling and making interior design choices. Your interior design theme is 'broken in a sea of plastic'.

TEN MONTHS

Baby can say 'NO'. The start of a lifelong love affair with the word.

ELEVEN MONTHS

Baby is relentless. By now you'll realise that you should have just got a dog that fits in a handbag.

TWELVE MONTHS

A magic time in a child's development – they can recognise television. Glory be to the power of television.

MYTHBUSTERS

MYTH: YOU CAN'T GIVE VODKA TO A BABY

Good vodka has been distilled many times over and is free from impurities so from that standpoint vodka is actually good for your baby. Most babies are fussy drinkers and won't drink vodka unless it's mixed with something that babies like. Thankfully, you aren't just an okay mother, you're also quite a good convenience store as vodka and breast milk makes a delicious morning pacifier for babies of all ages. This is not only an excellent sleep aid, it also starts working the liver muscle. Like all muscles, the liver gets stronger with use.

Myth status: BUSTED

BABY HEALTH

Babies get sick/dropped a lot so you'll constantly be seeking medical help/hiding injuries for the first year of your baby's life. Your baby is an accident waiting to happen. Don't worry too much about it. That's why they can't talk — so they can't tell people that you were busy liking Beyoncé's Instagram posts and not watching the baby.

DO YOU NEED A PEDIATRICIAN OR WILL 'SOME WEBSITE' DO?

Babies are gross. They are always sick like junkies or very old people. You will need constant medical advice. There are two ways of getting this. One involves an actual doctor and the other involves the internet.

Asking 'some website' is the modern way for mothers like you to get all scared and start self-diagnosing everything from carpal tunnel syndrome, to Lyme disease, to Spanish influenza, when actually it's just some banana that's dried and stuck to your baby's ruddy little face.

Let's have a really quick look at the two options:

Pediatrician

Pros: Prescriptions, diploma, magazines in the waiting room, kids that are sicker than yours will make you look like a decent mother, doctors have that soothing voice, chance to get some drugs.

Cons: Driving there, other sick people, boring, what if baby is actually sick — that's going to be expensive.

Some website
Pros: Way more interesting diagnosis, chance to buy some cheap Viagra.
Cons: Baby might actually be sick and die.

'HEY EVERYONE. I'M A MOTHER!'

Every time a baby is born, so is a mother. You can tell mothers from the other women because they are bedraggled, look like they are wearing an omelette as clothes and wear their eye shadow under their eyes. The way a mother talks, walks and stares blankly into space are also dead giveaways.

MAMA TALK

Talking like a mama is an important part of a new mother's development. Once mama talk is engaged, however, it's hard to switch off.

Mr Inanimate Object: Giving inanimate objects human traits is something all mamas do. It's not a car — it's Mr Car. It's not a table, it's Mr Table. It's not a crack pipe . . .

Ask the question, answer the question: All mothers need to ask a lot of questions that they then answer straight away.

'Who's a big boy? You're a big boy.'

'Where's Daddy? We don't know where Daddy is.'

'Why is Mama's life falling apart? You're why Mama's life is falling apart.'

Speaking in the third person: Speaking in the third person is something that evil geniuses, military dictators and mothers do. It will start when you are talking to your baby, but soon you'll be doing it all the time.

'Let me do that for you,' becomes 'Mama do'.

'I'm on my way,' becomes 'Mama come'.

'Give me one more piece of unsolicited advice and I'll lose it,' becomes 'Mama murder stranger'.

FACING BABY ADDICTION

Not all mothers become addicted. Those who don't tend to just exist in a state of blind panic. For those who fall prey to addiction, the obsession with their new forever-doll goes too far. Facing up to addiction is never easy but should be tackled head on. Look for the following signs:

If you're not showing someone a photo of your baby, you're taking one.
Shirking responsibilities, such as work, to spend time with your baby.
Neglecting your own appearance, but making sure your baby is 'clean and dressed'.
Being a hugely dull yawn festival whose lead act is 'Another Boring Anecdote About Your Baby'.

HOW 2

BABY-PROOF YOUR HOME WITH ONE ROLL OF DUCT TAPE

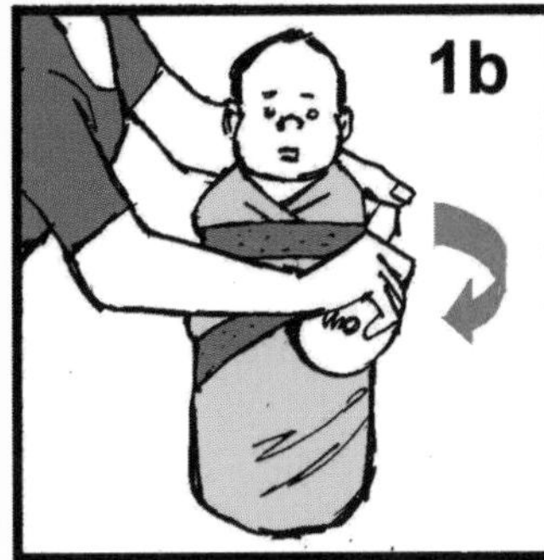

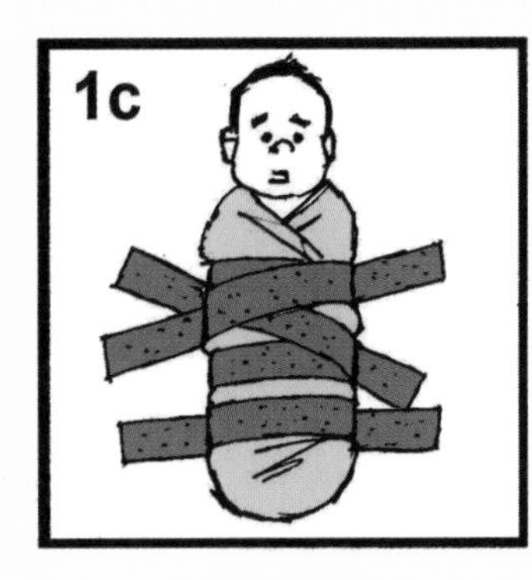

STEP 1a
Swaddle

STEP 1b
Tape

STEP 1c
Run

HOW TO TALK ABOUT SOMETHING THAT ISN'T YOUR BABY

Your baby is much like the approximately 125 billion babies that have come before it. Here are some things that ALL babies do. Please keep them out of social media newsfeeds and only discuss them with grandmothers and fellow addicts.

Sitting up: Could not be more basic. Definitely keep this to yourself.

Drawing with a crayon: Your baby isn't drawing. It's just banging a crayon onto a piece of paper.

Eating something sour: Again the internet killed our care factor. Try giving it a scorpion to chew on.

Sleeping on Dad: Not interesting at all. Two people sleeping. One is exhausted and looks terrible, the other sleeps all the time anyway.

Laughing at stuff: Okay, this might have been interesting 30 years ago, but since the inception of the internet, we have all seen babies laughing a million times. I've seen a bed of octuplets all cracking up *at the same time* so your ginger-headed chuckler ain't cutting it.

TOP TIPS

FOOD/SOLIDS

GRAZING BABY — HAPPY BABY

To make sure your baby is getting all the nutrients it needs let it graze on what you eat by having it crawl on the floor under you while you eat.

NANNIES AND OTHER DESPERATELY RISKY PRACTICES

If you've decided there's no way you can cope without help and you've decided to get a nanny — good for you. Your baby will probably grow up knowing who you are. And a nanny can be a fantastic scapegoat for any weird sexual proclivities your child may develop as an adult. But beware! Choosing a nanny is one of the most important decisions a new mother can make. *Because a hot nanny will ruin your life.*

IS YOUR NANNY UGLY ENOUGH?

Ugly is good. A hot nanny is a no-no. You aren't trying to scare your baby, just frighten your husband off. Here's what to look for:

Halitosis: If your nanny doesn't have bad breath, serve her plenty of salami and beef jerky, or lightly poison her with caustic soda in order to put in place a smelly force field that will kill most men's erections.

Age: Serious osteoporosis and degenerative muscle diseases don't usually kick in until women are in their seventies, and breasts start to lose their natural perkiness at around age 40. Based on these two factors, science tells us that the optimal age for still being able to fold clothes and carry groceries, but not run off with your husband, is 57.

FREE HELP

GRANNY VS GRANNY

The key here is to play your child's grandmothers off against each other and get them to outdo each other. If you work this dynamic correctly you may not have to actually raise your child at all. Make up the spare room and follow these simple steps:

Amazing things happen when the other mother is there: The baby smiled at her. It's definitely got a connection with her. What are you going to do about it, Granny?

'I couldn't do it without her': This needs to be said to BOTH grannies. The green-eyed monster will then visit within seconds, and you should have both grannies clammering to wipe poo while you nap.

'Number 1 Granny' mug: Buy one. Only one. Leave it in plain sight. They'll figure it out.

EXPLOITING THE CUTENESS OF YOUR BABY

Before you bombard the internet with thousands of photos of your baby so everyone can see the thing grow up in real time, people are going to give a shit and offer to help. Take them up on that help. Often. Don't be afraid to be specific with your requests.

HI WORLD! IT'S ME!

While you've been staring at your baby, the world has continued without you. Some things you'll recognise and some you may not. Here's a quick guide to assist with your eventual reintegration into society:

Tree: Totally safe. Home for birds. Some grow fruit.

Car: Used for travelling. Safe when still. Use caution if car is moving.

Mall: Malls are where our food and clothing comes from. Goods are exchanged for money.

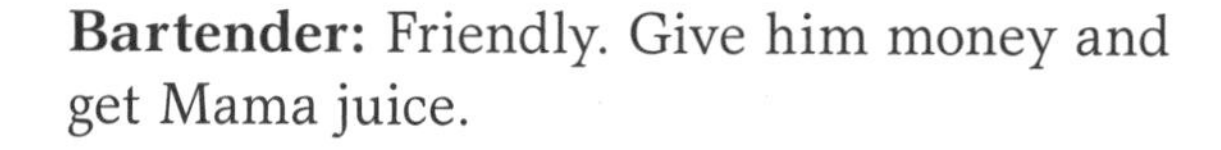

Bartender: Friendly. Give him money and get Mama juice.

Office: Bad place where dreams go to die. Stay away from there like you're French.

HOW 2

UNDERSTAND ADULTS

Adults use strange things called 'words', which they string into 'sentences'. But sometimes they don't mean what they actually say. Because you've been away for a while here's a quick look at what people mean when they say 'words'.

You look, great! = You look tired/fat.

Amaaaaaazing! = Not that amazing.

Wowwwww! I heard you were pregnant. = You still look pregnant even though you're not.

I've been meaning to call you. = I forgot you existed until I saw you and couldn't cross the road in time.

Let's catch up as soon as possible. = I'll forget you as soon as this conversation is over.

GOODBYE REAL FRIENDS – HELLO MOTHERS' GROUPS

Because you are now incapable of having a conversation about anything but babies, you need to find other people like you. Mothers groups might seem to be a collective of people you wouldn't normally piss on if they were on fire, but they are your people now. The only ones you have left.

MEET THE MOTHERS

There are five main types of mothers you'll meet in a mothers' group . . . and you'll be one of them.

The Know-It-All: 'Actually' is the first word that comes out of her mouth. The Know-It-All has the answers to questions you haven't even asked yet. And the answer will always begin with 'actually'.

The Mess: Sit next to this specimen and you'll feel like mother of the year. She hasn't changed her clothes for a week and is feeding the baby a rib bone.

The Me Me Me: Hasn't really embraced motherhood. Sees the baby as an accessory. Keep your baby away from her kids if you want to keep it out of rehab.

The Part Timer: Why is she smiling? Because she has a nanny. Why is she here? Because her actual friends hate her too.

The Won't-Make-It: Nervous. Skittish. Caffeine addicted. On the verge of tears. Fear behind the eyes. Sound familiar?

LIES MAKE YOU SEEM LIKE A GOOD PARENT

What might seem like chit-chat to the outside world is passive aggressive one-upmanship in mothers' groups. Chances are every time you leave the room someone will refer to your child as 'retarded'. Wait until your baby is asleep then make impressive developmental claims about them to the group. Just make sure they're all ones that can be rescinded by saying you dropped the baby while getting out of a moving car. Some examples are:

'I read to the baby every day': Don't use actual book titles, as one of the other mothers is bound to have read the book.

'I have to go. We have Mandarin lessons': Technically not a lie, if you teach your child how to peel a mandarin.

'She emotes at the level of a five year old': This is a fancy way of saying she has tantrums that are louder and harder to control.

EXERCISE . . . IN FUTILITY

Exercise is difficult and often requires effort and a change of clothes. This can seem too much and will often result in 'giving up'. To combat this, we've created a no-impact exercise plan where putting on the gear is around 89 per cent of the workout.

Sit up: The key to the sit-up is to sit . . . up. Find a chair and sit up in it. Do not tighten your core. Try not to slouch. If you do start to slouch, meh, what are you gonna do? Slouch.

Thumb lifts: Lifting your thumb requires no fancy equipment, except a television remote control. Lift your thumb to change channels or to increase the volume to drown out the screaming of your child.

Pointing: Pointing uses all the major muscles in the arm and hand in a very minor way. Do one rep for each of the following: Point at something you want. Point at the things that annoy you. Point to where you want people to fuck off to.

Yeah! Good workout, people.

CELEBRATE THAT MILESTONE FIRST BIRTHDAY

You made it. A year and the child is still alive. Great. Sorry to break it to you, but the first year is easy. Now the hard work starts. Pour yourself a drink and blow up some balloons. It's about to get screamy up in here.

TOP 5 FIRST BIRTHDAY THEME IDEAS

Birthday parties are more to show off to other mothers that you're in one piece than for the baby. You could hand the kid a ball of string and an empty chip wrapper and it would be in heaven. The last thing you want to do is organise a birthday party. So here are some thought starters for first birthday party themes that always work:

1. Other mothers drinking heavily
2. Pink shit everywhere!
3. The heavy silence of exhaustion
4. Corporate cartoon infiltration
5. Mayhem

SEX IN FRONT OF A BABY FREAKING YOU OUT?

If you ever want to have sex again, you'll have to learn to have sex in front of a baby. To get comfortable with being watched, a great option is to start by shagging in front of your cat or dog. Don't look directly at the animal. And definitely don't touch the animal.

OPINIONS ARE LIKE ASSHOLES — YOUR FATHER-IN-LAW IS ONE

You know who knows how to raise kids better than anyone? Your father-in-law. You'll find it difficult, but whenever he offers an opinion, try not to angrily say, 'Yeah, you did a brilliant job with your daughter . . .'

HOW LONG IS 'THE REST OF YOUR LIFE'?

The 'rest of your life' is how long you will be a dad. The rest of your life now means you carry even more responsibility during your relentless march towards death. There is some good news. Studies show that the rest of your life is a shorter time for dads than it is for men who can still do whatever they want whenever they want.

HOW 2

SLEEP IN THE TOILET AT WORK

Remember to set out-of-office reply.

ONE SUBJECT — FOREVER

You don't go to Pizza Hut and order a salad. You don't father a baby and expect to talk to its mother about anything else ever. Now you've had a baby, that's what you'll be discussing. There is no point trying to avoid this.

YOUR TODDLER

Baby's growing up. She's walking and exploring the world around her — and breaking it as she goes. She's got a vocabulary of around 350 words — but mostly just screams like a marauding Viking. She's meeting other little ones her own age — and biting them. The Terrible Twos usually only last 8765 hours 8 minutes and 1 second but sometimes they can last two years. If you have a god, now's a good time to pray to it.

Hello: Fear
Goodbye: Love

THE TERRIBLE TWOS

As your child starts to come 'online' and gain sentience, they also gain 'asshole status'. They think they're so big and smart and can do whatever they want. All it takes to disprove this is an afternoon and a front door left open. Here's what your next couple of years are going to look like:

12–14 MONTHS: YOUR TODDLER IS AS SMART AS A SPANIEL

Knows its name — and has started to ignore you when you say it.

Understands simple commands — and is either wilfully ignoring them or is a total douche.

Points to things it wants — which is everything bladed, scalding or made of angry cat.

Understands objects exist even when out of sight — so hiding while you cry requires more effort than just crawling under the table with a kitchen towel in your mouth.

14–18 MONTHS: DEVELOPING GROSS MOTOR SKILLS . . . REALLY GROSS

Up and walking . . . away from safety and towards everything sharp, high up and moving at 50 km an hour.

Wants to explore the world. Give it cab fare.

Does really terrible art and yet expects praise.

Says first words. You've been waiting for this for months. It'd better be 'MAMA'. Ungrateful brat.

Attacks other kids. Bites, scratches, growls. Blame the dog.

22–26 MONTHS: MEET YOUR TINY TEENAGER

Begins to explore genitals. For boys, this is the start of a lifelong pursuit.

Ready to be potty trained. Diapers start to look like they're from a retirement home for professional wrestlers.

Language good enough to be understood by strangers. Strangers are just people your toddler hasn't threatened yet.

Can undress itself. But still can't dress itself, making this a pointless skill.

Starts asking, 'Why?' a lot. 'Why are you always hugging your knees and rocking?'

Uses the word 'MINE' and understands the concept of self. But still won't take responsibility for the havoc it creates.

☆TOP TIPS☆

HIDING PLACES FOR BOOZE

While we are talking about you and your mental health . . .

The best place to hide little pick-me-ups is in plain sight. Right in front of everyone. Vodka in a water bottle on the home treadmill. Gin in a Sprite bottle. Put some carrots in your Jack Daniel's, pour it into a bowl and call it soup.

If plain sight is not your gig, try the standards: in cleaning product bottles, in pockets of winter coats, in the toilet cistern.

YOU AT 26 MONTHS

Sure, your toddler is developing and growing, but what about you? Let's look at what you can expect at 26 months:

You no longer care how you look.

You are entertaining thoughts of sex — they are very entertaining. They make you laugh.

You can recite 30 children's books without looking at them and do a very good horsey sound.

Your PTSD symptoms are manageable when treated with gin and tonic.

Your pre-pregnancy clothes fit . . . someone, somewhere, probably.

TODDLER MANAGEMENT

The next two years of your life should not be thought of as parenting, as much as corralling, negotiating and, in some cases, using sleeper holds.

DISCIPLINE AND YOUR TODDLER

If you only take in information from only one part of this book, make it this part. For the rest of our sakes.

Sometimes the time-outs you give your toddler do nothing but make it angrier, like a tiny *Incredible Hulk*.

Here are some enhanced ideas for disciplining the little monster:

1. Change the 'time-out room' to the 'time-out empty swimming pool behind the spooky house'.
2. Start using 'Lots More Tears' shampoo.
3. Make the kid play with 'Pieces of Elmo in a ziplock bag'
4. Make the naughty step the Mongol Steppe.

TOP 10 USES FOR ALL THOSE BOOKS YOU BOUGHT ON DISCIPLINING TODDLERS

All those books you bought on how to tame toddlers (including this one, but thanks for your purchase and your continued support) will provide you with no useful information. Here's how they can actually help though:

1. Letting your toddler tear the books to pieces will keep them entertained for ages.
2. Build a soundproof wall between you and your screaming toddler.
3. Bite into the book to muffle the sound of your crying.
4. Papier-mâché a happy mask to wear in public.
5. Use to start a nice house cleansing fire.
6. Let them 'accidentally' fall on you, putting you in hospital for a few days.
7. Balance the iPad on them while the toddler watches 'whatever it wants as long as it stops screaming'.
8. Use the pages to write SOS notes.
9. Hide a metal file in one and use it to escape.
10. Read the book on the plane as you escape, leaving your husband to 'raise' the child.

YOU SAY 'NO!' A LOT, BUT COULD YOU BE SAYING IT MORE?

You'll be saying 'no' more than any other word. You'll be saying it a lot. Up to 10,000 times a day. That's not enough. Employing our new technique will double the number of times you say no to your toddler each day.

Pre NO: The pre-emptive NO should be used the moment your toddler wakes. Then try one a minute until breakfast, before reducing to only once or twice an hour.

During NO: The most obvious time for NO to be used is while the toddler is misbehaving. In this instance, inhale and then scream one long 'NOOOOOOOOOOOOOOOOO' while shaking your head furiously.

After NO: This should be utilised between the pre NO and the during NO. For maximum effectiveness, whisper 'NO' into your toddler's ear while it sleeps for additional subliminal impact.

INFLICTING YOUR TODDLER ON THE WORLD

There comes a time in every parent's life when you must be prepared to be hated by the general public — and for good reason. It's time to take your toddler out. Those same strangers who told you how cute your baby was will now want to stab you in the eye with a dessert spoon.

SUPERMARKET TODDLER

Toddlers and supermarkets don't go together. This is a scientific fact. The evidence is all over supermarkets. 'Clean up. Aisle six,' is code for 'a woman has opened a vein with a potato peeler'.

If you must buy groceries, park your car in a shady spot. Ensure your toddler is firmly secured in its car seat, before handing it your iPad. Lock the car doors, then stroll into the supermarket to do your shopping, making sure to enjoy the wide aisles, pleasant music and air conditioning. If, when you return to your car, you see a crowd gathered attempting to unlock the door with a coat hanger, just use your remote to open the door. Then leave via public transport.

TODDLER HEALTH CHECK

Your toddler is growing, getting stronger and adding new weapons to its arsenal — think teeth, fists and ear-piercing screams. You know your toddler is in great health when everyone around you looks like they want to put it in hospital.

TEETHING

North Korea is developing a nuke and your toddler is developing its own weapons of mass destruction — teeth. These are the weapon of choice. For babies and toddlers alike. You will be bitten, the only questions are where, how hard and will blood be drawn? Teething only lasts for FIFTEEN DAMN MONTHS and so your little one will look like a drooling less intelligent Stephen Hawking that will want to put everything it sees in its mouth. Like its father.

New teething technology to the rescue: There are apps specifically designed for teething with many tips and hints, timers and recipes — some even have games. Simply download the apps to smartphone and then hand the smartphone to your baby and let her chew the shit out of it.

Vibrating Teething Tool: The rubberised surface and vibration of this Vibrating Teething Tool make it perfect to bring quick relief to any cranky teething toddler. And its size means it can easily be hidden . . . put away in the drawer next to your bed.

Defrosting pork or chicken: A great way to ease the pain of your child's teeth tearing through its gums. Give it the frozen raw pork and let the little mite defrost it in its mouth. Head to Foodpoisoning.com for handy tips on dealing with salmonella poisoning that may occur.

BREASTFEEDING A TODDLER WITH TEETH

Teeth are nature's way of telling you it's time to start weaning. Once your toddler has bitten you, breastfeeding becomes an exercise in fear. End the madness as soon as possible, before it gets a taste for human flesh.

Teething relief. For you. Forever.

POTTY TRAINING

Adults who were never potty trained and have poopy-pants don't do well in society, so this is an extremely important stage in your child's development. Here are some of the many available methods of potty training:

THE HAMSTER CAGE

Tear up all of the books on potty training you've bought and spread them throughout your house. Then once a week, sweep it all up and burn it.

THE DADDY

This involves reading in the toilet for a long time. Preferably a periodical, but in a pinch this method will work with the back of a shampoo bottle.

COFFEE AND A CIGARETTE

Using this method, your toddler will be on a bowel movement schedule you could set your clock to. Millions of overweight office workers can't be wrong.

THE BACKYARD

Slightly more contentious, this method requires the toddler to live in the backyard until it has the language skills to comply when told not to soil itself.

FIRST WORDS

Your toddler starting to talk is annoying, and it will force you into conversations about kitty cats and going bye-bye. A parrot would make for better conversation until the child is about three, and at least the parrot will call you pretty.

DEALING WITH THE BETRAYAL OF THE WRONG FIRST WORD

Occasionally a toddler's first word is 'Dada', and unless you're in a two-dad family, this is the greatest moment of betrayal that a mother will face. Unfortunately this disgraceful act of backstabbing connivance will have to be paid for by the father some day when he's least expecting it.

THE WORST WORD IN A TODDLER'S VOCABULARY

There is nothing worse than hearing a toddler say, 'Again!' Infinity is a toddler on a swing. Once your toddler learns to say 'again' it's time to up your wine intake. Unless you like doing the same thing 3000 times in a row, keep this word out of your toddler's vocab for as long as humanly possible.

THE QUESTION WITHOUT AN ANSWER

'Why?' is another path to madness. Entering into such philosophical discourse with someone with the brainpower of a terrier is not advisable. The answer to 'Why?' should always be, 'Because'.

'THAT WAS FUN. LET'S DO IT 300 TIMES' – GAMES WITH A TODDLER THAT YOU WANT TO PLAY INSTEAD

Toddlers are in constant need of stimulation and attention and this level of parenting can be a total drag. This is where games come in to fill the place of lightly banging your head against the wall and chewing a tea towel. Playing games with your toddler is a great way to stop the constant yelling and a brilliant way to teach your little romper-stomper about the world around him.

Peek A Booze: Cover baby's head with a soft blanket or duck behind a book and when baby can't see you take a big gulp of the strongest booze you have in the house. Then take off the blanket or pop up from behind the book and BURP as loud as possible. Continue game until one or both of you nap.

What your toddler will learn: That his mother is a good dancer.

Daytime TV: Turn TV on and place toddler and yourself in front of it. Sit motionless for as long as possible. Moving more than your thumb to change channels results in loss of points. Food may be eaten as long as it comes from the microwave.

Bonus round: Watching *Jerry Springer* counts as a crash course in raising kids.

What your toddler will learn: That sometimes cousins can also be brothers and sisters.

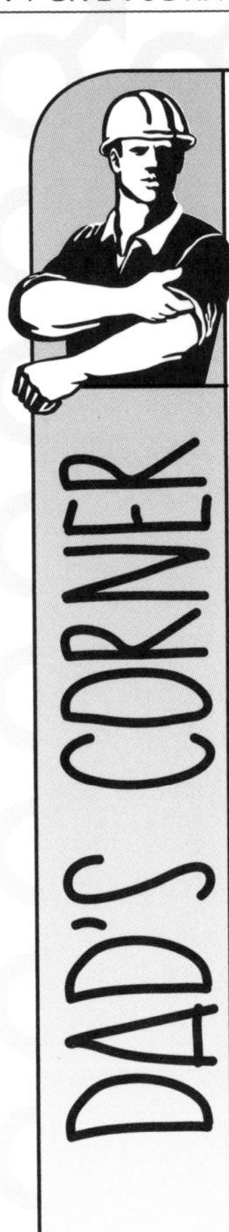

PLAN B

Faking your own death isn't as hard as you might think. It does however take commitment. Once you decide to free yourself you can't go back.

Record your toddler's bedtime performance, and keep the recording on your phone. If you feel like going home just play the recording again and again until the feeling passes, then get back to your new life as a boat captain, surf photographer or bar owner.

BROTHERS AND SISTERS

When your child is two years old, many people will tell you that having a second child is a good idea. As a father, you need to be vigilant in preventing this. Warning signs include:

Offers of sex: Why now? Because you're so sexy and she can't keep her hands off you? Don't fall for it. You're a fat schlub that hasn't looked worse. Remember that.

The toddler needs a brother or sister: You have siblings. You hate them. Move on.

Only children are creepy: Maybe so, but children who have been abandoned by their wayward and exhausted fathers are worse.

HOW 2

CAUSE INFERTILITY IN YOURSELF

3 hours of pain verses 30 more years of this crazy baby nonsense

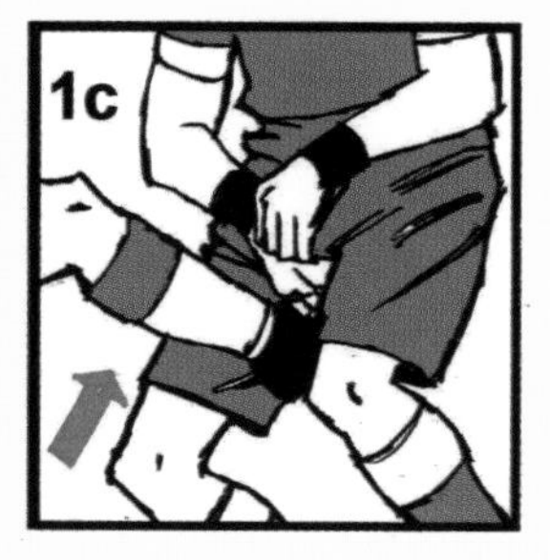

STEP 1a
Hold ball in front of balls

STEP 1b
Move ball, exposing balls

STEP 1c
Save money on future school fees

YOUR CHILD

Do you know where your child is right now? If you answered 'no' then reading this section is probably a waste of your time. If you answered 'yes' then you have probably already discovered the power of television. It might have been a bumpy ride to get here and there might have been moments when you've asked if it was worth it — the whole of last June is a moment — but the answer to that question is, of course, maybe. In this chapter we help keep you away from crack cocaine while you continue your 'parenting'.

You're not even nearly done raising the thing. Even though you feel like you've been doing this for years, and you have, you still have a long way to go before you can relax . . . or do you?

'HE'S NOT SHITTY. HE'S JUST "DIFFERENT"' — AND OTHER PHRASES TO EXCUSE YOUR SHITTY KID

Your shitty kid will constantly need to be excused and explained. Keep these excuses on hand, just in case

His father beats him.
He's on my drugs.
He fell over while he had a cotton bud in his ear.
He's just a loaner. My real kid's in the hospital.
He's a method actor and he's preparing for a role.

DON'T 'YOU CAN BE ANYTHING YOU WANT TO BE' YOUR KIDS

The world needs shelf stackers and forklift operators. Set realistic expectations for your kids. They can't be anything in the world. Statistically speaking, only about seven or eight people will be prime minister in their lifetime. That's way fewer than kids being born in the world.

MALL SECURITY AND OTHER CHILDCARE OPTIONS

Childcare is expensive and crèches are few and far between. However, hotels, malls, parking buildings and banks are everywhere you look. These institutions are gold when it comes to free childcare. Who better to leave your child with for a few hours while you run some errands? Just remember to act concerned when you return to collect your child.

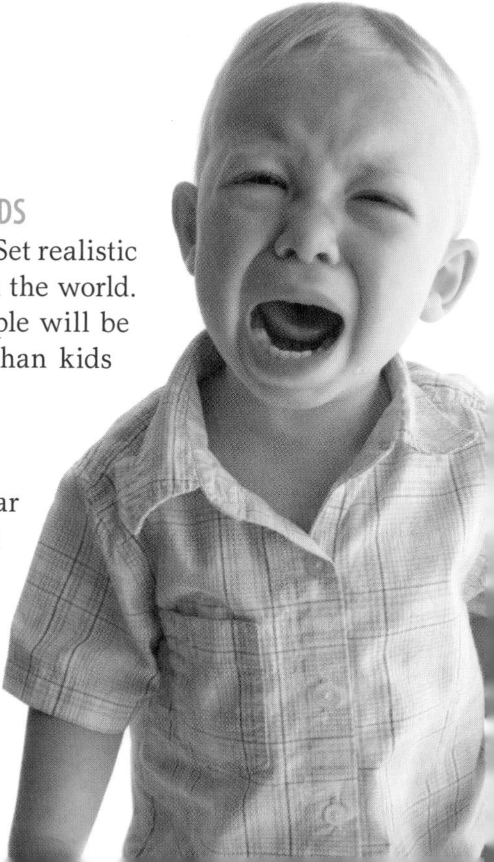

KEEPING YOUR RELATIONSHIP FRESH

It's hard to keep a relationship fresh with kids. Day after day of the same books, meals and songs, while you're the only one making any compromises. It's inevitable that things with your child will get stale. Here are some ways to keep your relationship fresh:

Go on separate vacations: Time apart is important. Make sure you put newspaper down, and leave food and water in a place your child can reach.

Give your child a new look: Bleached hair, piercings . . . or how about a bad-boy tattoo?

See other children socially: Other kids will give you some much-needed perspective.

Try out each other's interests: Would it kill you to eat a handful of dirt while you point at a dog every now and then?

KIDS ARE LIKE SPONGES — USE THEM TO CLEAN THINGS

Work gives kids a sense of pride and nimble fingers are excellent for sewing and putting little bolts onto little screws. Most kids can be taught how to clean an office and young ones may find it fun to work a vacuum cleaner. If your little one is still having trouble sleeping through the night, consider night shift.

KNOW YOUR KID TYPE

By now you'll be able to see the flavour of kid you've cobbled together. Maybe you're lucky and have Kid Classic. A nice normal-sized child of average intelligence with friends and a healthy obsession with boy bands and dolls. But chances are you've got a little piece of 'uniqueness' on your hands. Something fat, stinky, odd, creepy, possibly dangerous and downright unlovable. A true reflection of you and your effort as a parent.

KID CLASSIC

Basically a normal kid. Right down the middle. A tax-paying citizen. A consumer of things popular. Yay sports team. The Wednesday of kids. If this is your kid, well done — you've successfully shared the parenting load with TV. Both you and your child should be nicely numbfortable.

Cause: Modern life.
Fix: The inevitable death that faces us all.

FAT KID

Your fat kid doesn't want to do anything for two reasons. When you're a fat kid, doing things is hard. And then there's bullying. So much bullying. Pushing over a fat kid is a bully's bread and butter.

Cause: It's not glands — unless you're feeding him deep-fried glands. It's because you're feeding the kid like a trucker and he's got the lifestyle of a retiree.

Fix: Put a doughnut on a string and make him run next to the car or send him to Japan where he can become a sumo wrestler and bring much honour to your family.

CREEPY KID

Walking on tiptoes everywhere and laughing about nothing. Uses tiny handwriting to fill notebooks. Scribbles over the faces of people in magazines. You keep waking up to find him at the foot of your bed just looking at you.

Cause: Let's just chalk this one up to 'nature' not 'nurture' and walk away from the whole thing.
Fix: One small push on a boat trip . . .

DINOSAUR EXPERT KID

The kid that knows everything there is to know about dinosaurs or Boeing 747s or Egypt. Says 'actually' way too much and is starting to drink coffee.

Cause: Ask your kid what the cause might be — he's the expert.
Fix: Try forcing your kid to play with dumber kids. The dumb kids should knock some sense out of him.

QUICK CHECK

YOU'RE NOT STILL BREASTFEEDING, ARE YOU?

If the child can actually ask you to nurse using a well-constructed sentence, it's time to stop breastfeeding. Kids shouldn't be saying, 'I'd really like to drink some milk from your breast.' Or anything like that.

It's freaky. Stop it.

SICKLY KID

Always sick and leaking snot all over everything. Gasping for a lost inhaler and sitting inside with a sun allergy while everyone else bullies the fat kid.

Cause: Look to your weak husband. This is why you breed with the fittest of the species. It's survival of the fittest not survival of the most interesting at dinner parties.
Fix: Let natural selection run its course.

STARTING SCHOOL

School is a huge milestone in your child's development, mainly because your child becomes someone else's problem for eight hours a day. And the blame shifts from you to the system. These are heady times indeed. Why not light an 'incense cigarette' and watch a movie that doesn't have the word 'princess' in the title.

ESSENTIAL GEAR FOR THE FIRST DAY OF SCHOOL

The first day at school requires some equipment to make sure that it runs smoothly. Here is an exhaustive list that should help make that first day as smooth as it can be for you:

Balloons (if possible, filled with nitrous oxide)
Streamers
Punch bowl (large)
Vodka
Gin
Lemons
Disco ball

HOW ANY SCHOOL CAN BECOME A BOARDING SCHOOL

Schools are filled with responsible and knowledgeable adults who will do a better job of raising your children than you ever would. But not every school is 'officially' a boarding school. But don't let that stop you giving your child the best upbringing you can. Simply drop your child off at the school gates equipped as if they were going to camp. Pack them a sleeping bag, cooking utensils, some trail mix and a can-do attitude. Then drive away, change your SIM card, home address, town and possibly country. After a couple of years, return and collect your child after their immersive education, ready to assimilate back into family life.

COMPETITIVE DRESSING FOR THE SCHOOL RUN

The school run has long been the domain of competitive mothers. The key thing to remember here is NOT TO GET OUT OF THE CAR. This is standard behaviour. But if you do have to leave the confines of your KIA Sport (as good as the Range Rover but better for the environment . . . cough) then it's best to dress either very up or all the way down — and always have a story.

Imaginary meeting: Dress for the meeting you wish you were at, not the meeting you don't have. This is a great way of wearing your best garb and putting on too much make-up without looking like you're trying too hard.

Imaginary gym session: Dress down in hoody and sweatpants for a reason, not because you've only just managed to claw your way out of bed. It's because you're going to the gym. 'Can't stop and talk about my kid sucking at French. Personal trainer is waiting.'

Imaginary wedding: Win at school run dressing by putting on a formal gown, and pretending you're going straight to a wedding. It's not because the only way to make yourself feel halfway decent is to pull out every last stop.

GIRLS' SPORTS — HOLY SHIT — SO BORING

For a father, having girls is just one disappointing situation after another. But nothing is more disappointing than girls' sport. It's an exercise in self-deception and denial. Girls' sport is like watching paint dry . . . if it was special paint that dried slightly slower than normal paint and needed way more encouragement or it might start crying. The only exceptions to this rule are tennis and beach volleyball.

GAME ON

DRINKING GAMES TO MAKE WATCHING GIRLS' SPORT FUN

Drinking will become key for any father watching girls' sport. Here's a drinking game that should help you eke some fun out of an afternoon watching your girl try to throw a softball or kick a soccer ball.

1. Daughter cries and doesn't want to go because of the uniform: **drink beer.**
2. Daughter misses ball with foot: **drink beer.**
3. Daughter just sort of talks and hangs out with friends while game continues: **drink beer.**
4. Daughter doesn't touch the ball once: **drink beer.**
5. All girls get MVP trophy at the end of the game for 'trying hard': **drink beer.**
6. Coach has to stop some little diva crying: **drink beer.**
7. Final score is zero to zero: **drink remaining beer.**

THE COST OF HAVING CHILDREN

As well as the lazy $300k your kid has cost you in diapers and Tickle Me Elmos, you've paid for them with so much more.

Hair: Stress kills follicles and now you look like you're wearing a skin yarmulke.

Car: Mini van mini fun mini stereo mini freedom mini penis.

Sex life: Gone in a flurry of sleeplessness and baby body embarrassment. Now the most you'll get is a begrudging hand job, which you have to clean up yourself.

Abs: You used to have a six-pack now it's gone. You used to go to the gym, now you go to Princess Movement Dance Class. Now you have a belly that's as soft as a baby's bottom.

YOUR CHILD ON A BUDGET

Disneyland: Tell your child you'll take them to Disneyland if good behaviour is forthcoming. After months of good behaviour, drive them to a demolished factory and tell them Disneyland must have been pulled down.

Dog: Negotiate the procurement of a dog for your child. After a few months of good behaviour 'buy' your child a dog. Then a week later, tell your child the dog has run away and collect the reward for returning the dog to its owners. Depending on the reward you should break even after feeding the dog for a week and have enough left over for ice cream.

ARE YOU DOING ENOUGH PRETENTIOUS JUNK?

Doing pretentious junk is key to being considered a good dad. Ask yourself — are your activities organic and gender neutral? Do they involve music even when music has no place in the activity — jazz funk fishing class anyone? And are they eye-wateringly expensive? Do they make you culturally uncomfortable? If you answered yes to these questions, you're being a good dad.

If you don't have pretentious junk near where you live, why not start some pretentious junk of your own as a money spinner. Remember. Just pointlessly add music.

PARENTING

Parenting is a team effort. You are '(insert surname) United'. You're not a fancy premier league team, so you don't need a uniform. You're already easily identified by the stained, messy and manic exteriors you share. You are playing a game called 'raising a child' and there are no rules, no trophy, no cheering crowds, no half-time show and no advertising revenue. There are only 5 am starts, and the occasional head butt or groin kick. But this is what you wanted, so put on your game face and get on with it.

PERCEPTION PARENTING

Research suggests that you don't have to be a good parent so long as people think you're being one. The people you most need to fool are other parents. Teachers know what type of child you have created and, unless you are on a plane or in a restaurant, strangers don't see you any more. You are as invisible as you feel thanks to your hair, the stains and the pushchair that you are hiding behind. To seem like a good parent try the age-old technique of lying. 'I can't come to your barbecue because Angelica has piano lessons.' 'Little Jon is doing "bueno" in Spanish — for someone so young he's really picking it up.' 'My youngest hasn't stabbed his sister in the thigh with a pencil so many times lately.'

Perfect perception is perfect reality.

THERAPY VS PARENTING

Start putting money into a therapy fund for your child now. Therapy makes your actions someone else's problem and is a far easier solution than consistently 'turning up' to do the job of raising your kids. Artist alert! Many successful artists often cite childhood trauma as being fuel for their success — after extensive therapy, that is.

THE 30/70 RATIO — NO PARENTING UNTIL THURSDAY LUNCHTIME

Apparently 30/70 is the magic parenting ratio. You can do a good job 30 per cent of the time and your child will still survive, albeit with sociopathic tendencies. But that's a small price to pay for not having to parent until Thursday lunchtime.

If you're okay with that, then the 30/70 principle is for you. You can make sure the child is alive for 30 per cent of your time, leaving you 70 per cent of your week to do whatever it is you like doing, which we can guarantee isn't parenting.

THE 'ONE-TWO PUNCH' OF PARENTING

Because you're a parent, your life is going is to be an average one . . . at best. 'Quickly' and 'badly' are your two new best friends. They'll give you time to do stuff for yourself. How do they work?

Quickly: The key is to rush through everything. Don't take time to do anything properly. Why cook a meal when you can get it from a drive-through window? Don't read a book to your child when a DVD can do the reading for you. Don't explain things to your child, just yell at them. Much faster.

Badly: Doing things badly is so easy it's almost fun. Skim read the homework, sort of get them vaccinated, sometimes bathe them, occasionally attend parent–teacher evenings, use most of the bolts when assembling new bunk beds.

PARENTING IN PUBLIC

At home you have the bribes and waterboarding equipment you need to control the little dissidents, but parenting in public is a whole new ball game. Public is full of people who:

Don't have kids and will judge you.

Have kids but pretend theirs aren't hateful little gnomes so will judge you.

As a result, you need to adopt strategies to 'parent' under the watchful eye of some jerk-off strangers.

Chloroform on Teddy: Douse a favourite teddy in chloroform, then remove it from a plastic bag in times of tantrum or panic. 'Night night, angel.'

Low, threatening growl: Stoop to child's eye level, bare your teeth and growl something terrible and painful involving death. Drag your index finger across your throat for extra effect.

Walk away: Simple and non-violent, just walk away and pretend the child isn't yours. Write the child's name and address on the inside of their clothing and they should eventually make their way back to you unharmed.

Spock neck pinch: One pinch and the child goes down. Invaluable for the busy parent. Painful and incapacitating for the wayward child.

WIN AT YELLING

There are many theories about yelling at your children but if you are yelling effectively you should be able to avoid hearing any of them. Yelling is a great way to let a child of any age know that their life will be in danger if they don't comply. Yelling can also be used to communicate with other adults who may displease you by offering opinions on your parenting.

TOP 10 PARENTING PHRASES YOU'LL NEED

Kids respond best to threats and constant repetition. These are some phrases that you should learn and use often to make your children pliable:

1. Do it or you'll make Santa commit suicide.
2. Stay in bed or the monsters will swarm on you.
3. Where's your iPad? Go get your iPad. iPad time.
4. You used to have a brother, but we sold him because he did that.
5. Your father wants to beat you, but I'm talking him out of it.
6. That book you want me to read again got stolen.
7. How was work today?
8. Listen, kids like you disappear everyday and no one bats an eyelid.
9. Don't tickle-tickle your boy-boy or I'll burn your hand with a birthday candle.
10. Mama drinks because you are boring.

MYTHBUSTERS

MYTH: A DOG CANNOT RAISE A CHILD

There have been some reported cases where children have been abandoned and wild dogs have raised them. However, the children have become more like dogs than people. But it could have been the fault of the dogs — maybe they just weren't cut out for parenthood. The fact that these wild dogs kept a child alive means it is possible. Find a suitable pack by heading to the shittier parts of town with some dog food. Put the food out in an abandoned building and wait. The stray dogs will turn up and then it's just a matter of leaving your child in the capable paws of the pack.

Myth status: BUSTED

PROFESSIONAL ATHLETES AREN'T BORN THEY'RE COERCED

No one loves their mothers more than professional athletes. Every successful athlete has a mother in a mansion driving a pink SUV and getting their nails done in between going to games and the Maldives. It's a very real career path for you to follow. All top athletes start very young and are gently and lovingly forced into a sport that eventually causes them to be a bit mentally imbalanced, but makes their parents a lot of money.

Is your baby small and weird looking?
Top jockeys can earn up to $4 million a year.

Does your baby fall over a lot and cry all the time?
Soccer players can earn millions each year.

Does your baby bite?
Top boxers earn hundreds of millions, before being rendered unable to talk.

Does your baby reach for your breasts at inappropriate times and have an obsession with its own genitals?
Golfers have been known to earn up to a staggering $1.3 billion over their careers.

HOW MUCH TELEVISION IS NOT ENOUGH TELEVISION?

Studies show us that kids are spending up to six hours a day watching television. What can you do to increase that by at least double, so you get at least 12 hours a day of not being asked questions?

IS ONE TELEVISION IN EVERY ROOM ENOUGH?

One TV set in every room is only going to increase your child's TV consumption by half. You need to ask yourself if you want to hear your kids asking for things. If the answer is no, double up the TVs.

TELEVISION AS AN ALARM CLOCK

Some people wake up to a juice. Some people wake up to a dog. Your kids wake up to a blaring television, and you'll get to wake up whenever you damn please.

TELEVISION IN THE CAR

TV sets can easily be installed in the headrests of your car or SUV. Then all you need to do is put the kids in the car and drive it 500 metres or so from the house. Call a designated driver for the trip home though, we both know you're drunk.

KIDS NEED BOUNDARIES

It's long been said that children need boundaries, and I'm not talking soft emotional or behavioural boundaries. I'm talking about real boundaries. Here are the best boundaries I have seen:

RAZOR WIRE

The favourite of penitentiaries all over the world, razor wire provides a reliable boundary, which will maim rather than kill. It's good for your kids to get used to the sight of this stuff now so it's not such a shock later.

ELECTRIC FENCES

What works for dumb animals like cows and horses will surely work for your kids. Small shocks 'modify' your child's behaviour making them easier to manage.

MOATS

When you absolutely have to keep your kids in, or out as the case may be, nothing works like a moat. Fill your moat with something that bites and you've got something that could keep a teenage boy who's drunk five beers out of your home.

WRITING OFF THAT FIRST CHILD

The first child is always a write off. Nobody expects you to actually raise the child into a productive adult. You don't give a Ferrari to a new driver and expect the car to come back without some serious damage done to it. The best you can hope for is that the child doesn't end up getting you put in prison.

Don't be afraid to just quit and stop caring too much about what your first child does. Learn your lessons and move on to making the next child, and this time try your best not to make the same mistakes.

A PARENT ALWAYS CHOOSES NATURE

Nature vs nurture is a debate that's probably been raging since an early child kept scribbling over cave paintings and defecating in the wrong corner of the hovel. Yet every parent knows the answer to this question is nature. That's because nature can be blamed on your parents, and on genes that have been handed down by them. Nurture, on the other hand, is a direct result of your crappy parenting.

KEEPING GRANDPARENTS HEALTHY

Sure it would be great to inherit a house you could sell and maybe some cash if there is any, but your parents are the best free resource you have to shoulder most of the burden of your terrible kids. Making sure they don't die should be one of your primary concerns.

Don't die yet! Please don't die yet!

MAKE THE PERFECT SCREAMING INTO PILLOW

Also works as a smothering pillow. #justsaying

EXERCISE

Encourage your parents to go to the gym, do water aerobics, take up cycling and become more active in general. As your kids get older, the grandparents will need to be more agile and strong to control them.

DIET

Heart disease is a killer of old fogeys, so make sure they are eating right. Send them scary articles that you find online and tell them about kale.

EXPENSIVE DOCTORS

Your parents deserve to spend a lot of money on good doctors, so you can make sure they'll be around until your kids are teenagers and can join a street gang. Sure it's money you won't inherit, but not having to raise your own kids is worth it.

BACK TO WORK – DEALING WITH THE GUILT OF NOT FEELING GUILTY

Because you're not a billionaire, you will have to go back to work and place your children in childcare to be raised by strangers. You'll drop them off in the morning and pick them up at night and probably only see them for a couple of waking hours – and it will be frickin' awesome!

Not feeling guilty is a normal response for working parents, but you need to look like you feel guilty. Here's how:

LIE

Lying about being miserable to be away from your kids is important because people are judgmental bastards.

PHOTO ON YOUR DESK

Even though it can be hard to look at your kids, having a photo on your desk will make you seem like less of a monster.

WORKING LATE OR WORKING WEEKENDS

Even though you'd like to volunteer to do both you can't. You have to choose one.